Million Dollar Smile
Save Your Teeth and Your Wallet in Friendly Nicaragua

Eva van Loon

The Pack Press

Copyright 2012 Eva van Loon

The Pack Press
6799 Cranberry Street
Powell River, BC V8A 3Z3
www.thepackpress.com

First printing, 2012

No part of this book covered by copyright hereon may be reproduced or used in any form by any means, graphic, electronic or mechanical, without prior written permission of the publisher, except excerpts in a review of 250 words or less. Direct your requests for photocopying any part of this book to the publisher.

Cover design by Katje van Loon
Photos by the author

National Library of Canada Cataloging in Publication
van Loon, Eva, 1948—
      Million Dollar Smile: Save Your Teeth and Your Wallet in Friendly Nicaragua

Nonfiction
ISBN 978-0-9813592-5-0
      1. Title. 2. nonfiction. 3. dentistry. 4. Nicaragua. 5. dental tourism. 6. Leon, Nicaragua. 7. dentures.

Table of Contents

I Wuz Bad	5
Isn't Nicaragua Dangerous?	13
Why Nicaragua?	15

    15 • Economical
    18 • Dollarized
    19 • Accessible
    23 • Networked

But I Don't Speak Spanish!	25

    25 • Fawgeddabahdit!
    26 • Spanish in Three Days
    30 • Online courses
    30 • Good little books and gadgets
    31 • Enroll in a Nica Spanish School

How Can I Find a *Good* Dentist?	33
How Much Will It Cost?	45
How Do I Plan My Trip?	48

    48 • How Long Should I Plan to Stay?
    48 • Where Should I Stay?
    53 • Should I Rent a Car?
    53 • What about Insurance?
    54 • What Should I Pack?
    58 • Mouth and Body Prep

What Else Can I Do While in Nicaragua?	62

    62 • Trips and R&R
        62 • **In Leon**
        63 • **Near Leon**
        66 • **Beyond Leon**
    72 • Business or Research
    73 • Learning
    73 • Volunteer

What Should I Watch Out For?	75

    75 • Trucks!

- **76** • Thieves
- **78** • Sidewalks
- **80** • Misdirections
- **81** • Snakes
- **82** • Dysentery
- **82** • Chileros

Are There Downsides?   84

- **84** • Return trips
- **84** • You may never leave

Will You Be My Guide?   85

- **85** • Twist my arm
- **86** • Toothy Vocabulary
    - **86** • **Spanish to English**
    - **87** • **English to Spanish**
- **89** • Resources
    - **89** • **Managua:**
    - **89** • **Leon and Las Penitas:**
    - **90** • **Granada:**
    - **90** • **Ometepe:**
    - **90** • **Upcountry:**

See You in Sunny Nicaragua!   91

About the Author   92

I Wuz Bad

"Next time you have cancer, nobody will treat you with a mouth like that!"

Those frightening words emerged from the well-groomed facial orifice of a doctor—or was it my dentist? No doubt he meant well but he scared me. It's bad enough to face the prospect of surviving another round of cancer—it's little short of terrifying to think that you'll be on your own for treatment options.

People who survive their sixties are more likely to reach a ripe old age.

I read that somewhere. It makes a certain sense: if the body is going to fall apart because of sins committed in youth, isn't that failure likely to show up after five or six decades? Half a century of poor health habits must surely take its toll.

I reflected. I was in my sixties, and old age or something worse was definitely stalking me.

I wuz bad, as they say. If you asked my body, I had definitely been a bad girl for years—not loud-rock-concerts-and-fast-food-and-drugs bad, but stress-and-overwork-and-accidents-and-I-need-a-stiff-drink bad. When the body wasn't even half-grown, it had been subjected to a rash of radiation treatments on the back of the neck for, of all things, a little eczema. (Such craziness was not uncommon in the medical field of the Fifties.) The eczema had survived the radiation. My sense of smell and my thyroid had not.

Neither had my teeth. They went soft and mushy. It had been a fight for decades to keep my fangs functioning. Now my mouth sported four broken teeth, punctuated by blackened cavities. A crown had come loose and a gigantic amalgam filling had fallen out—lucky I didn't swallow the ugly thing. A quarter-century ago, my front choppers had been fixed up with plastic after a fall that broke them off about a centimeter from the roots. Over the years, the plastic had yellowed to new-moon shade, with a hint of green, almost a match, but not quite, for my darkened, left-over natural fangs. A neat little triangle had recently chipped off one of them.

Not exactly kissable. Just call me Lady Snaggletooth.

It wasn't just the hag-like appearance of my mouth that was troubling. Eating wasn't easy any more. It required the fine art of discrimination among (1) foods that might break more teeth, (2) foods that would insist on hanging around in the canyons of my dentition, and (3) foods that could be gratefully tongued down after just a mild whack or two from the front teeth. The molars were not up to an omnivorous diet anymore, either.

Constantly, I picked at my teeth—or flossed to remove food bits, an ever more daunting exercise. I worried about my breath, remembering a poet friend whose romantic affect was completely ruined by the stench of his rotten teeth. I didn't want to put clients and friends through that!

Then there was toothache. I knew it was vital to keep my body alkalinized to damp down inflammation and avoid cancer and diabetes, but all the baking soda and magnesium chloride in the world could not put an end to the nightmare of the recurring toothache. You know how it is: when you're doing toothache, you're not doing anything else—like work. Paradoxically, the less I worked, the less money I'd be able to scrape up for the dentist!

With the able help of baking soda and oil of oregano, I was able to kill every toothache within forty-eight hours. Yet these darned teeth wouldn't stop plaguing me. Someday soon, I would be forced to visit the dentist. And I could guess what dentists would say.

It's too bad you don't have insurance.

Yeah, well, tell that to the divorce court.

We have a monthly payment plan and we do the work as soon as it is paid for.

Right. By which time I'll be eighty-five years old.

You're a bit old for implants, especially with the bone and gum loss you've allowed to happen.

I get it: it's a two-tier system—and anyone as far gone as I am stays in the bottom tier.

Yes, we can do implants where you've lost your crowns. If uncomplicated, they're four thousand, one hundred dollars (plus twelve per cent tax, of course) and we can subtract the hundred and fifty that your health plan will pay for an extraction. At the same time we could give you new crowns—they're only a thousand or so. Apiece.

I will be working to age ninety-two to pay off my new mouth!

Most dreaded dentist's opinion of all? *It's time for a denture.*

For some people, a denture is a relief and no big deal. *Yank out the offending beasts and let's start fresh*, is their attitude. For me, a denture seems proof positive of irreversible senectitude. Both my parents—and a step-parent—had dentures, whose wretched clicking sounds at every meal I will never be able to scrape out of my ears. In their last years, I assisted with moving those disembodied teeth in and out of place a zillion times and never got past loathing the process. The pitiable sunken cheeks of my mother without her teeth brought tears to my eyes. No, dammit! I was not going to cave to a denture—if I had to end my life with just a scattering of semi-functional teeth in my jaws, let them at least be my own!

Of course, I did seek out dentist services. When a crown that a certain local dentist had installed came loose, I called him for an appointment. It had taken me two years to pay the more than $900 for that crown, just four or five years earlier. Weren't the darned things supposed to last a decade or more? A flurry of flustered discussion at the other end of the line resulted in the startling information that appointments were now being made months away but, the receptionist assured me, I could have the first cancellation that came to the office. *Don't call us; we'll call you.*

Yeah, sure. Apparently there were no cancellations for the entire ensuing year. Dentistry must be good business in Canada.

A second dentist in town seemed eager to see me. He yanked the offending crown off its weak foundation, leaving me with a small canyon with mini-rebars sticking up—fun to clean, that was! Brusquely, he informed me an implant was not for me; he favored a campaign of extractions and dentures.

I hoped a trip to the Big City might prove more useful. It certainly proved more seductive. At a cushy new office with free parking under the building, I almost relaxed right into a lifetime plan of eternal dental care, everything included. I let them x-ray me and put a temporary top on the latest broken tooth, they were so nice and the office was so soothing. Beautiful music and inspiring videos played constantly. Two implants; no problem. Being broke, I would enjoy slightly lower rates than the insured.

Several hundred dollars later, I staggered happily out of that poppy field, convinced that my teeth could, after all, be saved—I could have a new mouth. At a price. An imprisoning price, I found on doing the math. All I had to do was make the $250 trip to the Big City every couple of weeks and promise to pay. Forever.

The work itself now waved a bling price tag. Two implants...eight or nine crowns...in the twenty thousands? Each trip would mean giving up paid working days, plus travel costs, and I would have to figure out where to stay...say twenty trips? At a conservative two hundred and fifty dollars per trip? Another five grand on top of the dental costs.

Maybe I could take out a mortgage on my hobbity little house?

The situation was serious. Every dentist I'd seen had commented on the effects of a broken-down mouth on general health. In particular, I was told that chemo or radiation treatments for cancer, should it pay me a return visit, would not be done unless my mouth was able to combat the inflammation that invariably arises under such treatments. If that wasn't enough to scare the hell out of me, I was told about the link between receding gums and heart attacks, bone loss and a host of degenerative diseases.

And then there's oral cancer—one is not immune just because one doesn't smoke. Something told me that if my mouth was an inflamed mess, it was a prime site for cancer to find a new home...next time.

A little web surfing washed up a heap of information about oral cancers, which can occur anywhere in the mouth—lips, tongue, gums, cheeks, the palate or throat. Mouth cancers most often develop in smokers and drinkers—even more so if one indulges both those habits. Although I didn't fall into these categories, I could relate to the list of symptoms to watch out for: white or red patches in the mouth, sores that won't heal quickly, ulcers, inexplicable lumps, loose teeth, numbness or pain. Even a painless lesion can apparently harbor cancer.

Thanks to my baking-soda habit, I hadn't had any of those white or red patches for a long time, but this is still scary information for people who have already been through cancer once. If you are concerned enough about your teeth to read this, you need to know this horror story, too. In fact, everyone should know this, the younger, the better.

The Mayo Clinic on its website[1] lists an array of nasty effects on your system by what it is pleased to call poor "oral health."

What conditions may be linked to oral health?

Your oral health may affect, be affected by, or contribute to various diseases and conditions, including

- **Endocarditis.** Gum disease and dental procedures that cut your gums may allow bacteria to enter your bloodstream. If you have a weak immune system or a damaged heart valve, this can cause infection in other parts of the body — such as an infection of the inner lining of the heart (endocarditis).

- **Cardiovascular disease.** Some research suggests that heart disease, clogged arteries and stroke may be linked to oral bacteria, possibly due to chronic inflammation from periodontitis — a severe form of gum disease.

- **Pregnancy and birth.** Gum disease has been linked to premature birth and low birth weight.

1. http://www.mayoclinic.com/

- **Diabetes.** Diabetes reduces the body's resistance to infection — putting the gums at risk. In addition, people who have inadequate blood sugar control may develop more-frequent and severe infections of the gums and the bone that holds teeth in place, and they may lose more teeth than do people who have good blood sugar control.

- **HIV/AIDS.** Oral problems, such as painful mucosal lesions, are common in people who have HIV/AIDS.

- **Osteoporosis.** Osteoporosis — which causes bones to become weak and brittle — may be associated with periodontal bone loss and tooth loss.

- **Alzheimer's disease.** Tooth loss before age 35 may be a risk factor for Alzheimer's disease.

- **Other conditions.** Other conditions that may be linked to oral health include Sjogren's syndrome — an immune system disorder — and eating disorders.

How can I protect my oral health?

To protect your oral health, resolve to practise good oral hygiene every day. For example,

- brush your teeth at least twice a day;
- replace your toothbrush every three to four months;
- floss daily;
- eat a healthy diet and limit between-meal snacks; and
- schedule regular dental checkups.

Also, watch for signs and symptoms of oral disease and contact your dentist as soon as a problem arises. Remember, taking care of your oral health is an investment in your overall health.

The Huffington Post ran a story about the influence of poor oral health on cancer, documenting the findings of a study published in the BMJ Open online journal. The study examined 1,390 people between 1985 and 2009, asking them a number of questions regarding cancer factors, including oral hygiene. After twenty-four years, 58 patients had died. Thirty-five died of cancer-related causes, and across all 58 deceased was one common factor: a higher amount of dental plaque than those in the study who didn't die. The authors of the study say, "Based on the present findings, the high bacterial load on tooth surfaces and in gingival pockets over a prolonged time may indeed play a role in carcinogenesis."

It's not been proven yet, and the authors do call for further research into the subject. Still, the findings are pretty sobering.

Then The Mouth Doctor[2] explained the connection between oral health and the rest of the body, otherwise known as "my life"—now I knew I was one of millions potentially in deep, deep trouble.

PANCREATIC CANCER - People with poor oral health have a 63% greater chance of contracting Pancreatic Cancer.

Cancer of the pancreas is a disease in which cancer (malignant) cells are found in the tissues of the pancreas. ...The pancreas has two basic jobs in your body. It produces juices that help you break down (digest) your food, and hormones (such as insulin) that regulate how your body stores and uses food. The area of the pancreas that produces digestive juices is called the exocrine pancreas. About 95% of pancreatic cancers begin in the exocrine pancreas. The hormone-producing area of the pancreas is called the endocrine pancreas. Only about 5% of pancreatic cancers start here.

PANCREATIC CANCER AND ORAL HEALTH

According to an article recently published in the Journal of the National Cancer Institute, men with poor oral health have a significantly increased risk of developing pancreatic cancer over those with good oral health.

[...] Pancreatic cancer is the fourth leading cause of cancer deaths in the United States. The majority of patients are diagnosed with pancreatic cancer once it has spread from the pancreas to distant sites in the body, a stage referred to as metastatic pancreatic cancer. The reason that the majority of pancreatic cancers are diagnosed at such a late stage is that the disease usually causes no symptoms until it has spread. As well, there are no universal screening methods for the disease.

Due to the lethal nature of pancreatic cancer, understanding risk factors that contribute to its development is critical. [...]

Researchers from Massachusetts and Puerto Rico recently conducted a

---

2. www.mouthdoctor.net

> clinical study to evaluate the potential association between oral health and the development of pancreatic cancer. [...] Overall, 216 patients were diagnosed with pancreatic cancer during the study.
>
> - A history of periodontal disease increased the risk of developing pancreatic cancer by 64%.
> - Among individuals who had never smoked, the risk of developing pancreatic cancer more than doubled for those with a history of periodontal disease compared to those with no history of periodontal disease.
> - The greater the severity of periodontal disease, the greater the risk for developing pancreatic cancer.
>
> The researchers concluded that periodontal disease significantly increases the risk of developing pancreatic cancer among men. These results provide more data to support a relationship between good oral health and overall health."

Did you note the survival rate for this cancer? About five per cent? This is the cancer that famously gives you about five weeks' warning of the end of your life—and you might have prevented it by fixing your mouth? Scary!

Since my successful cancer surgery, I'd had two mysterious attacks, one of which mimicked the onset of pancreatic cancer perfectly. Ordinary life—and work life—had evaporated swiftly during these attacks. The eventual diagnosis was not cancer but a dead thyroid or an impaired endocrine system—whew! Nevertheless those days of mild terror taught me a valuable lesson. Had my illness proven to be pancreatic cancer, I might have had only weeks of life left in which to accomplish my dreams and duties—because of a disease I might never have contracted if only I hadn't procrastinated for years on taking care of my teeth!

It was time to do the previously unthinkable—become a dental tourist.

And just how was a little old lady who earns less than twenty thousand a year (including pension) going to pull that off?

But I did! With this little book, you can, too.

See that toothy grin on the next page? My mouth is eight shades whiter and can eat anything. Best of all, now I'm not afraid to smile. At my life. At the world. At you.

Isn't Nicaragua Dangerous?

No.

That's the simple answer. Nicaragua feels safer than Mexico, Costa Rica, or Guatemala to me and now enjoys a growing reputation as the safest country in the region.

I've never once felt threatened in Nicaragua, in two month-long trips. Mind you, everyone cautions visitors not to walk alone at night in a big sprawl of a city like Managua or touristified Granada—good advice in any big city, even in the US or Canada. As an older woman on her own, however, I've joined New Year's Eve crowds in the colonial city of Leon, past midnight, without a qualm. If anything, some additional respect seems to be extended to little old me—thanks to the "old" part. In beach towns like Las Penitas, I've been to known to stroll on the beach or street at most any hour to find that their most distinctive quality is silence—the original silence of the Earth. I remember a night spent on the beach with visitors and locals, watching a rare eclipse, without a concern for safety in the darkness. Beautiful.

Politically, Nicaragua is now close to boring. The political climate Carrie Snyder so eloquently describes in her book *The Juliet Stories* has evaporated. The wars and revolutions are long over although the many statues, murals and memorials to the 1959 fallen martyrs and heroes of the revolution and the Eighties' Contra war remain. Everyone now seems to belong to the same nondescript national political group. I've asked people what differences they saw after the revolution or the Contra wars in the Eighties, and the answer is invariably, "Things are *mas o menos* (more or less) the same."

I would feel far less confident on my own in Mexico, Costa Rica, or parts of Guatemala, countries I've visited in the past two decades. Even parts of downtown Vancouver, where I practised law for fifteen years, are nowadays no place to walk alone to your parked car.

This is not to say pilfering is not rampant. On each of my trips, a friend came to pick me up from my overnight-arrival hotel in Managua. On the first visit, his truck mysteriously lost its extra front lights in the quarter hour it took to collect me—despite the vehicle's being guarded in the parking lot by my friend's rather fierce wife. On the second visit, I needed a quick shower in the morning, having been too tired on my arrival the night before. I threw back the pristine shower curtain to find…no taps!

Someone had absconded with the shower taps, and some of the copper wiring from the bathroom's electrical switches for good measure. The hotel made good, of course, and I got my shower in a fresh room. I'll bet some heads rolled over that incident and can only hope justice was done, rather than vengeance.

Nicaragua is poor. Currently it vies with Honduras and El Salvador for the title of Poorest Country in Central America. A friend I visited there paid her staff three hundred dollars a month—for all three! Yet the price of gas is comparable to that in Canada (currently almost six dollars per gallon). When people are this broke, their sense of poverty can only deepen by watching visitors flaunt expensive jewelry, watches, or equipment. Leave your classy stash at home.

Nicas may be poor but they are not miserable. Far from it. You will encounter far more smiles, street parties and greetings per square mile than at home, and the Canadian reputation for politeness will seem undeserved after you deal with the courteous Nicas for a few weeks.

Nicaragua values family life highly and lives to socialize and party at the lightest excuse. During September and October, the Feast of the Virgin was held, a heavy-duty excuse for fireworks and processions as early as five in the morning and as late as dusk, complete with enthusiastic firing of rockets which make a satisfying roar and pop, sometimes all day. A kid's birthday party, especially a *quinceanero* (a girl's fifteenth birthday), is a great excuse for a block party, complete with traffic police to steer vehicles elsewhere. Political appearances, student celebrations, harvest celebrations, New Year's—you name the occasion and you'll find it unfolding on a plaza with loud music, street food, photo kiosks, kiddie rides, souvenirs.

Despite all the parties and celebrations, however, the University students are more earnest and dedicated than any I've met for years in North America. After family life, education of all kinds is sought after and highly prized.

Just once, I was nearly cheated 200 *cordoba* (about eight dollars) by a taxi driver. To this day I'm not sure whether he didn't know how to make change or he thought I wouldn't notice. He didn't object to repeating the counting process three times, however, and I received the proper change—I left him a tip as a reward for honesty, however reluctant it may have been. That was my closest brush with larceny in Nicaragua other than the disappearance of one chocolate bar from a friend's refrigerator. I didn't sense that Nicas think the *gringo* owes them a living or that the tourist is an easy mark. *Straightforward* describes most of my dealings with people in Nicaragua. A notable exception is the *chilero*...more on that interesting topic later.

Why Nicaragua?

A private room for $4 and a chance at an excellent prince to boot. Hard to turn down!

Economical

The number-one reason for visiting Nicaragua is money—the huge amounts you will save. You can have a holiday here when you couldn't possibly afford to go anywhere else. You can live here very well even on a slender Canadian pension. And the dental fees run ten to twenty-five per cent of the fees in North America.

On seven hundred dollars per month, you can cover rent, utilities, dinner out, cleaning service in, medical costs, bus travel and entertainment. If you add wine or beer to your meals, throw on an extra hundred or so per month. That's how inexpensive Nicaraguan living can be.

I met a pair of Canadians in Leon who retired early—before entitlement to their scrawny pensions—to rent out a modest house in Leon and get their health back. They're doing it, on about twenty-five dollars per day. He, according to her, looks ten years younger as well as many pounds lighter and they are enjoying truly golden years.

Contemplate the wall paintings while waiting for your delicious, freshly cooked meal by Jack the Pirate, your Canadian chef.

Jack the Pirate said goodbye to his job in Vancouver when 9/11 happened. After years as a successful restaurant cook in several Latin America locations, he settled in Leon, Nicaragua, where he'll serve you a satisfying dinner of tasty fresh food for as little as four dollars in his *cafetin*, which sports just three or four dining tables—and a pool table. Jack's restaurant employs a couple of locals but he keeps life simple. Before opening the doors at four p.m. six days a week, he lives the good life at a nearby establishment, enjoying his passion, pool, with visitors, expats and locals. It's a hard life!

Here are some day-to-day prices for Nica prices and services. During my 2012 trip, I paid $6.40 for a consultation at a private medical clinic, pennies per pound for bananas and local greens, $3 per pound for grass-fed beef, $3 for full breakfast, $10 for a handmade hammock, $3 busfare from Granada to Leon, $9 for a pair of new sandals, $22 for a beautifully stitched leather cowboy hat, $4 for the movies (air-conditioned, with subtitles), and a whopping $4 for a glass of good wine with dinner. When I needed the hospital, the x-rays and the TLC were free of charge; the *jefe* (chief) refused to take a donation. During a run-in with the runs on my first visit to Nicaragua, a laboratory analysis and medicine which ended the problem in twenty-four hours came to…$1.65. (Yes, for both.)

The leather hat will bring out the cowgirl in you!

The only expensive items I've found in Nicaragua are books—almost all are imported from more expensive countries—and gas, which runs about the same as Canadian prices, currently almost six dollars per gallon.

Of course, you are most interested in dental prices. Details are further on in this book but for now, let me say that I estimate saving at least sixteen to eighteen thousand dollars on renovating my mouth in Nicaragua and that's after including airfare, accommodation, and insurance in my Nicaraguan dental costs. The dentists' fees themselves range from ten to twenty-five per cent of North American fees.

If dental materials are imported from the US or Europe, naturally that percentage will fluctuate according to the cost of the materials. This happened with the tooth-whitening kit used for my mouth, the very latest thing from the US. In North America, that treatment costs between five and eight hundred dollars. Because of the exorbitant cost of the kit, my dentist had to charge three hundred—still a wonderful deal for me! I'm eight shades whiter.

The difference between North American and Nicaraguan costs is nicely illustrated by the startling disparity in the price of the aftercare products prescribed by my dentist for my bone graft. This protective stuff comes in two forms: goop and mouthwash. A month's supply in Nicaragua costs under ten dollars. In Canada, the stuff must be imported or made: the cost is eighty-five dollars per month, plus tax, if you please. Over nine months, that's less than ninety dollars in friendly Nicaragua versus seven hundred sixty-five plus tax in good old Canada.

I flew to Nicaragua and back for less than the difference in those prices.

Dollarized

There are two forms of currency in virtually universal use in Nicaragua, *cordobas* and US dollars. This means you can arrive with a wad of US dollars and pay for everything in cash without the hassle of changing money.

Money-changers stand on central street corners offering to change your money, presumably for a rate slightly better than the bank rate. I've never used them because there's simply no need. All you need to know on landing at Managua is how many *cordobas* fit into a dollar (twenty-four-point-something at time of writing, which makes a *cordoba* a little less than a nickel) and you can easily calculate the cost of anything and pay in either currency. Often prices are listed in both dollars and *cordobas*, anyway. It couldn't be easier.

You will need cash because many smaller places of business do not offer service for *tarjetas de credito* (credit cards). Even my dentist had no credit-card facility. Having at least some travel sense, however, I didn't wish to carry around the several thousand dollars I planned to pay him; so the solution was simply to visit a large bank's ATM every few days and pull out more cash with my debit card. The downside of this was the five-dollar charge by my home bank for every withdrawal; the upside was freedom from worry over stashing large amounts of cash anywhere. Now that I know the quality of my dentist's work, however, next time I'll simply bring the cash with me and pay him up front.

This easy money system doubtless arises from Nicaragua's long, convoluted history with American interests, which goes back a couple of centuries. Before the Panama Canal was built, there was a strong drive, headed by American businessman Vanderbilt, to put the canal through Nicaragua. A river emptying into the Caribbean could link to the largest freshwater body in Central America, Lago Nicaragua, and then a canal could be dug down to the Pacific. When you see Lago Nicaragua for the first time, you will be so glad the Canal never happened here—it would have ruined this beautiful country. The dispute over the canal plan, however, turned Nicaragua into the true Wild West for a time. At one point, the country was even ruled for nine months by General Walker, a genuine American wild man and astonishingly successful soldier. Perhaps he's the one who should be thanked for preserving Lago Nicaragua as the must-see ecological and cultural destination it is today.

Research Nicaraguan history online. It makes fascinating reading.

Accessible

The only bad news on accessibility is that wheelchairs will have a very hard time in Nicaragua. The sidewalks are so atrocious in places that you simply have to laugh—I began taking pictures of the most egregious examples of these Torts Waiting for a Victim. (See pages 20-21.)

Municipalities can get away with this because Nicaragua does not boast a civil personal-injury legal system like that in Canada, the US, Australia and parts of Europe. If you are restricted to a wheelchair, you can still have your mouth fixed in Nicaragua but you will have to take taxis pretty well everywhere.

Street traffic can prove difficult in many countries, such as India or Mexico, which are otherwise attractive medical-tourism destinations. The traffic rules differ from those at home, and cows, burro carts, and an unquenchable entrepreneurial spirit takes over what should be your part of the street, in the form of hawkers and kiosks selling everything from underwear to music to lunch.

The roads and sidewalks vary wildly in type, quality and dangers, often without warning. That's nothing new—seasoned travelers have learned how to assess their ability to cope with the differences. While the *carreteras* (highways) in Nicaragua are great, streets, many of them centuries old, are…well, endlessly interesting, to put it kindly.

Oops! A pile of dirt looking for a purpose as we wheel around the corner. Time to wander out into the street—carefully.

Why is this lady walking in the street where she has no right of way? Because you must be under three feet tall to use this sidewalk without bonking your head—that's why!

A shrine to San Diego, patron saint of Altagracia, straddles the median on the handmade highway into town.

A well drained street in Sutiava, the indigenous suburb of Leon. Chickens, puddles, kids and dogs do the traffic-calming here.

In all other ways, however, it's hard to beat the accessibility of Nicaragua.

First, you don't need a visa before you fly and flights are easy, frequent and serviced by major airlines. The main change-over points are Houston or Miami. Typically, a flight runs from Vancouver in the early morning to Houston and then direct to Managua by mid-evening, with the reverse for the return trip. Sometimes you trip over a deal, like my extra-special $262-return airfare on my most recent trip. Wow! Even with $325 tax and $250 or so in top travel insurance, boarding the dog cost me more than basic travel expenses.

Second, no jet lag. Nicaragua is an hour later than California and British Columbia; two hours earlier than the eastern seaboard (without considering Daylight Saving Time). That's not only easy on the body but also easy on any work or communications you may want to carry out while in Nicaragua.

Third, you can get home from there without a plane. In the unlikely event of not being able to access a flight, there are land-travel options. You can drive to neighboring Costa Rica, for example—many people do. You're not marooned, as many travelers were stuck on the Hawai'ian islands after 9/11, for example, and you're not limited in your travel options to just Nicaragua.

Fourth, traveling around the country is easy. Despite the horrendous cost of gas, a thriving *taxista* industry ushers and guides visitors around the country.

For trips between towns or touring the country, you could rent a car yourself but only if you're not shy about dealing with *vaqueros* and their herds of wild-looking cattle using the highway, horses cropping the margins of the roads, burro carts, overturned oxen carts, and the inevitable police, who may ask for strange and previously unheard-of paperwork or fees. If your Spanish is truly fluent and you have a hankering to go where no *gringo* has gone before, this may seem like your only choice. Driving happens on the right-hand side of the road, after all, and some hotels will have a *parqueo* to safeguard your car at night. However, I can think of many situations that would make me wish I'd just hired a driver, instead.

Taxi rides within town are usually twenty cords, as they say—less than a dollar. Drivers may pick up another passenger going the same way, which you should regard as a fresh opportunity to practise Spanish with the ever friendly Nicas. For travel out of town, consult a travel outfit to join a guided trip in a van—they're quite economical and a lot of fun—or plan your own itinerary with the aid of a *taxista*'s published list of rates between centers.

For example, I hired a *taxista-con-guia* for the whole day on the island of Ometepe for fifty dollars (one of the best days of my life!). The driver-guide was suggested by our hotel owner. Later, I hired another *taxista-con-guia* for a long, two-day round trip into the mountains for about one hundred ten. I also paid his hotel room (a big eight dollars) and meals (ten for dinner, breakfast and lunch) and added a tip. Looking back now, I can hardly believe I saw Matagalpa and Jinotega for two days for about one hundred fifty dollars, and Granada and Ometepe for around the same. A similar trip between Vancouver and Powell River would cost two to three times as much, although the gas cost is no higher in Canada.

For short trips, the so called chicken buses are a perfectly good option provided you have little or no luggage. The seats are ratty but people are friendly and I saw not a single live chicken. Buses run frequently and cost what Nicas can afford—a dollar or two, usually expressed in cords (*cordobas*). The bus from Leon to the beach towns of Poneloya and Las Penitas costs twelve cords now—a jump of two cords since 2011. Fifty cents to get to your beach holiday. If you're into adventure or saving money and Spanish is rolling around on your tongue, buses are the way to go.

Networked

In an unobtrusive restaurant in the center of little Altagracia on the island of Ometepe in the middle of Lago Nicaragua, my guide and I had a happy time becoming friends on Facebook on my laptop. Meanwhile, he was in constant contact with his job via cellphone, and I had a local cellphone, too. Back in Leon, my daughter and I held long business meetings over Skype.

Yes, cellphones and wi-fi are everywhere in Nicaragua. Internet cafes punctuate every major city street, too. Well...that's a bit of an exaggeration but you won't have to go a single day without electronic contact.

Two companies vie for your cellphone business, Movistar and Claro. Buy or borrow a phone; it's too cheap to bother with installing a local chip into your own phone. Ask about rates for calling home (US or Canada) before you choose—those rates can be a lot cheaper than the roaming charges on your own phone.

So many locals have cellphones that it took four weeks to discover that my hotel's land line could not contact cellphones. No doubt this anomaly will disappear in the near future.

I was glad to have my laptop along, because that meant I didn't have to find a favorite internet café everywhere I went, nor did I have to wait for an available computer. At some hostels, however, since many guests are backpackers without their own computers, the computer facilities are so convenient, one leaves the laptop in its case. At the other end of the internet spectrum, our hotel halfway up the mountain on Ometepe did not have wireless and my

Poneloya host's house lay in a small ravine where wi-fi could not penetrate. There are many homes and small establishments where wi-fi is iffy at best or non-existent.

But I Don't Speak Spanish!

Fawgeddabahdit!

Forget about it! Seriously, don't let a lack of Spanish keep you from taking advantage of dental care in Nicaragua. Just as there are places on the planet where, despite speaking the lingo pretty well, you are given short shrift because your accent gives you away as a member of a group that's not especially popular, there are lots of places where people will bend over backwards to help out the foreign traveler bewildered by the local language. Nicaragua is one of the latter.

Remember just these two rules to help break the communication barrier: (1) politeness pays and (2) every Nica wants to learn or practise English.

Politeness is a cultural practice throughout Latin America that in Nicaragua goes far beyond the Canadian. Use the phrases "Por favor" and "Gracias" until you think they'll wear out—they won't.

Add "Con mucho gusto" (With much pleasure) and "A la orden" (You're welcome) and you've won over most people.

Add "Busco" (I'm looking for) and "Quiero" (I like, I love, or I want) or the more polite "Quisiera" (I would like to have) and your listeners will know you need something.

"Me gusta mucho" means you like it (without needing to specify just what it is you like).

"Donde esta el bano?" is that all important question, "Where's the bathroom?" (Don't forget to tag on "por favor".)

Greetings happen all day long in Nicaragua with anyone whose eyes you meet. "Buenos dias" in the morning is often shortened to "Buen dia." "Buenos tardes" often becomes "Tardes" in the afternoon and the evening "Buenas noches" often drops the /s/ sound.

For North Americans all this spontaneous courtesy seems forced at first but try it in the interest of general improvement of international relations; you'll quickly grow to like it and you'll meet many more locals.

Flashing your phrase book doesn't hurt, either: when people see you trying to speak their language, they are emboldened to meet you half way with their English. A small notepad and pencil is a great addition, since so many Spanish words resemble their English equivalents; often your listener can decipher your scribble to recognize what you need. Use the dental vocabulary near the back of this book to help you communicate with your dentist.

When Nicas realize that a visitor doesn't speak Spanish, they will trot out all the English they have—and some they've made up, with often hilarious results—if you encourage them. A good sentence to throw in where appropriate is, "You speak English well." When they reply with a half-protesting thank you, model for them by replying, "You're welcome."

Every day I spent in Nicaragua, I met at least one person who wanted to practise English with me, from the high school English teacher who shared a cab with me to the night staff at the hotel. Some wanted me to teach English to him or her, to the family, to the community. Since half my professional time is spent teaching language and I regard teaching as some of the greatest fun to be had in the world, I started thinking about how I could speak English in a way most useful to them.

In case you are of similar bent, to keep the Spanglish conversation going, I suggest

(1) keeping your sentences short and simple, with the subject first and the predicate second,

(2) enunciating clearly but not too obviously, and

(3) repeating the correct form of their own English sentences with a question mark at the end as if asking for clarification.

For example, on being asked, "We go come to hotel tomorrow?" you would model, "We are going to come to the hotel tomorrow? Yes, let's meet at the hotel tomorrow." Usually the speaker will repeat the sentence the way you said it, and you can see it being filed away in the language-learning area of the brain. Wow. You did a little something for somebody—and didn't even need to speak Spanish to do it.

Spanish in Three Days

If you simply must have some Spanish under your belt before venturing into Latin America, there exists a highly successful course that teaches you to communicate happily in Spanish in just three days. In fact, on the afternoon of Day 1, you will be using full Spanish sentences and your pronunciation will echo that of a native-born Spanish speaker—your pronunciation coach. You will have so much fun and experience so much learning in this course that you will be inspired to go on learning Spanish with other courses or just by practice in daily life.

This course was devised by Merri and Gary Scott, a successful and generous couple whose newsletter about Spanish, learning, health, Ecuador, international living, investment, spirituality, shamanism, music, cuisine and just about every other topic of enduring interest to humanity has garnered an online audience of over 32,000 people.

You read that right: thirty-two thousand people.

A linguist, Merri Scott was one of the few individuals outside Bulgaria credentialed in a method of learning a second language we now call Super-Learning. The Super-Thinking + Super-Spanish course first integrates the brain. Students learn better with relaxed concentration. Then the course teaches seventeen simple lessons so they know over four thousand words in Spanish and can use them to create sentences. In this way, they can communicate in just three days.

The Scotts are now training Super Teachers in this method (I'm one of them) to disseminate learning Spanish by this method. The course is not dirt cheap but you'll see from the testimonial raves that it yields big results even for people who thought they had tried everything. From personal experience I can corroborate the exceptional effectiveness of the course.

There is no name for the Scotts' interest group and no membership or initiation procedure or fee. If you choose to sign up for the Scotts' daily newsletters (reading them is like having a little daily holiday), you'll soon discover that there are ways to make this learning very cost-effective. Here's a sample from one of Gary's newsletters in August, 2012. The testimonials speak for themselves.

Does it sound impossible to learn Spanish in three days?

It is in the traditional way of learning a language.

However, there is a scientific method of learning, proven and described in numerous best-selling books, that creates educational jumps by making education natural, easy and fun. This course works because it is education without stress!

Part of the Super Thinking method was created and refined by the Bulgarian educational master Georgi Lozanov, who transformed the entire Soviet educational system to such a degree that this third-world Union beat the USA into space.

Merri was lucky to be one of a handful of students outside Bulgaria who were allowed to be taught this system in the early Seventies. She has been practising this unique and remarkable form of education for four decades.

Lozanov's teachings form one of seven keys used in the course. These seven include:

1. 17 lessons teaching the student 4005 words that are the same in Spanish and English so there is no memorization of vocabulary.

2. Lozanov's teaching used certain forms of Baroque music throughout because the brain likes hearing it. This causes the mind to open and relate to pleasure.

3. Using a wave system to improve vocabulary so students can hear themselves and others speak words without fear.

4. Developing confidence by having students create Spanish sentences in the first three hours so the process is more meaningful.

5. Staying totally in the infinitive so there is no conjugation.

6. Using relaxation sessions and humor to keep the students in a state of relaxed concentration, the most effective state for learning.

7. Getting students to speak well enough in three days to mentally and verbally create sentences that keep Spanish active in the mind.

A Livescience.com article helps explain why this course works. Jeremy Hsu, LiveScience Senior Writer, in "CIA Seeks Anyone, Anyone Who Can Speak 2 Languages", shows what has been wrong with traditional Spanish courses and why the Super-Thinking tactic is perfect for this program.

Many Americans don't learn a second or a third language from birth. "In U.S. education, we don't develop early bilinguals," Catherine Doughty, a language expert at the University of Maryland, said at the American Association for the Advancement of Science (AAAS) conference in Washington, D.C. She and other speakers described the typical U.S. second-language program as a series of disjointed classes where students often repeat what they learned before. Robert O. Slater, director of the U.S. National Security Education Program, invited the audience to imagine math [programs] where the middle school says, "We don't have any idea about what you studied," and so students must learn it all again. He suggested, "It's the same with high school."

This is why traditional Spanish courses often do not work. They create two obstacles up front: conjugation and memorization of vocabulary. Super-Thinking + Super-Spanish avoids both these obstacles.

The article reported, "Repeated studies of French-language students showed that their brains responded differently to real French words compared with fake words after just two weeks of classes, even if the students themselves could not tell such words apart."

"From knowing nothing to a little bit, [there are] huge changes in the brain," Osterhout pointed out. "[From] knowing a little to knowing a lot, [it is] much more subtle." This is why Super-Thinking + Super-Spanish works. The three-day-course focus is entirely on making the huge change and ignores the subtle. The three-day course prepares the learner to speak Spanish immediately and then make subtle changes in day-to-day life.

Neither age nor language proficiency seem to predict how quickly immigrants pick up English. Instead, the fastest learners are those who show the greatest motivation to learn and a willingness to use English at every opportunity despite being bad at it (at first). This three-day course gets the delegates speaking and thinking Spanish all the time so they can use Spanish every day, communicating even from the beginning. In this way, the education proceeds even when Spanish is not being spoken.

Just read a few of the many raves we receive from delegates who have learned from these new teachers how to communicate in Spanish.

"[T]he eye-opening, mind-expanding Super-Spanish course last weekend in St. Louis surely shows me the opportunity exists to expand my horizons. Besides the course's having a lot of nice people to learn our new language with, the methods Merri and you developed proved to be just what you said they would be. We all relaxed our way to new learning. I feel so very comfortable with the basis of my new language skills that I know I will be spitting out great Spanish sentences by the time I reach Ecuador in October. --D.M."

"I finished Super-Spanish Super-Learning. My high expectations for the course were exceeded. After three days, I can speak Spanish in complete sentences. In simple conversations, such as buying groceries or ordering a meal, I can make myself understood. I think that's incredible!"

"I liked the laid-back yet professional approach. I highly recommend this new, relaxing method of learning Spanish. I feel a lot more confident in the delivery of my words and sentences. It was taught in an excellent and very professional way."

You can sign up for the Scotts' newsletter at www.garyascott.com. Drop Gary and Merri a line (gary@garyascott.com) and let them know you found their site in this book. The newsletter will tell you where and when all the Spanish-in-Three-Days classes will be held for the next few months, including any of mine.

Online courses

If you can't join a group of people learning Spanish and are forced to go it alone, nowadays there are fortunately plenty of online courses which promise to immerse you in real, everyday Spanish as well as teaching you grammar. I cannot endorse any of these as I don't know them or their results as I do *Spanish in 3 Days*, but here are two methods that look interesting: the Pimsleur Approach and Synergy Spanish Systems.

When you look these individualized courses up online, you will probably see dozens of Spanish courses ranging from free to hundreds of dollars. Some of them will come with discs that you can play in your car for practice, which to some weird people (like me) constitutes fun.

Be sure to select courses that teach Latin American Spanish rather than European Spanish. There are significant differences in pronunciation which could alter how easily your Spanish is understood. And you have enough to think about!

Every country in Latin America has its own way of speaking Spanish. For example, Nicas often don't pronounce the /s/ in words, or elide (skip a syllable). They'll understand your Latin American Spanish with your North American accent, but understanding them may prove a little difficult until you get used to it.

Good little books and gadgets

Call me old-fashioned, but I still like to pack along a real book on the language I'm trying to learn. I don't cart along a fat dictionary and a phrase book any more but *Breaking Out of Beginner's Spanish* (Joseph Keenan, 1994) still makes a galvanizing breakfast read. Like so many other books, it is also available on e-readers. Today that's the easy way to take along your entire library of books to learn Spanish—just put the dictionary, the verb book, and the idiom book all on your e-book reader.

You can't whip out your e-reader when it's back in your hotel room while you're trying to give the taxi driver directions, however. I recommend a purse-sized phrase book until you've memorized everything in it. The one I love is

Berlitz' *Hide this Spanish Phrase Book*. The publisher says, "Travelers will be able to speak Spanish like locals by using the easy-to-read pronunciation. *Hide This Phrase Book* includes conversation starters, ATM and bank info, hostel expressions, fun entertainment options, making friends with the locals and more. Also included is a two-way dictionary, featuring slang terminology."

Perhaps equally useful is *Dirty Spanish: Everyday slang from What's Up? To "F*%# Off!"* by Juan Caballero (Ulysses Press, 2011), which is less dirty and more useful than it sounds. It has chapters on Party Spanish, Horny Spanish, Hungry Spanish, Friendly Spanish and more. I guarantee you will laugh yourself off your breakfast chair at the amusing expressions, not to mention you might get some use out of being able to translate the "cool slang, funny insults, explicit sex terms, and raw swear words" that may invade your ears. *Cuidate* (take care), however: I did not hear much swearing in Nicaragua compared with some other Latin American countries (which shall remain nameless). You don't want to provoke anyone.

On my most recent trip, I took along a new gadget, a twelve-language translator, battery-operated. Palm-sized, light, and rather dumb, it proved useful enough for me to take it along again next time—or perhaps I'll find its smarter brother somewhere. Such toys are often on special at big-box stationery stores.

If you own a lightweight laptop computer and you intend to stay more or less put in Nicaragua, by all means take it along. Aside from playing movies with Spanish subtitles and bringing your work with you, it will let you carry on with your online courses, add your new Nica friends to your online community and get involved in social networking in Spanish.

Enroll in a Nica Spanish School

If you learn better in a group, the many Spanish schools in Leon and Granada may be your ticket to early fluency. The site Transitions Abroad[1] says, "It is no secret that the best way to learn to speak Spanish is full immersion—go abroad, live with a non-English-speaking family, take classes every day, study, practice, make mistakes, then repeat these last three steps until your brain feels like refried beans. Nicaragua is a prime location for your language-learning travails: A cheap and safe nation where, for about US$250 a week, you will get 20 hours of instruction, room and board with a family, trips, and activities. In comparison, a similar program in Spain would cost at least $500 a week.

"With few exceptions, most schools follow the same basic structure involving a combination of language instruction and cultural immersion activities. That means two to four hours of class in the morning, followed by community

---

1. http://www.transitionsabroad.com/

service activities or field trips in the afternoon. Most schools are flexible and offer one-on-one instruction, or teachers best suited to your Spanish level, even if your only word is *'hola."*

I've taken such courses in Guatemala and they are, indeed, a great educational and cultural bargain. Keep in mind, however, how much of your time you will be at the dentist's office, and whether there are time conflicts. Your mouth is the primary reason you're in Nicaragua. Spanish can wait.

How Can I Find a *Good* Dentist?

For me, choice was simple and I pass it happily on to you. I had a referral from Gary and Merri Scott for a dentist in Ecuador but realized prices in Ecuador could be higher than in Nicaragua. I had a second referral from an old friend, a Canadian now living in Leon, Nicaragua. I'd seen three dentists in British Columbia and wasn't happy about the prospects with any of them (being ignored, being treated as a bad old girl, or being treated as a pension fund, however nicely). So, when I received a call from yet another friend in Leon inviting me to stay with her and three days later stumbled over a return fare to Managua for the princely sum of two hundred sixty-two dollars (plus tax), it seemed the Fates were conspiring to put little old Lady Snaggletooth into a Nica dental chair.

And why not? I thought. I desperately needed a holiday and wanted to poke around in Latin America a lot more. I could let the dentist start with those nasty black spots on my front teeth, and if I liked his work, we could proceed with the heavy-duty procedures. How bad could it be? Zillions of Canadians seemed to be reporting satisfaction with dental work done in Mexico every winter—I would hardly win a prize as an intrepid dental pioneer by doing this.

A memory returned of my dental saga at age twenty, when I sought relief from agonizing pain from the exact middle of the face to the rear of the right jaw. You would think any dentist would check out the wisdom teeth on a client of that age with those symptoms, wouldn't you? My handsome dentist, then a recent graduate who had probably contributed substantially to dental students' proudly held reputation for partying and chasing girls, didn't think about my wisdom teeth until after he had had extracted a perfectly good bicuspid of mine. Hence today, instead of still having twelve of my own complete teeth, I have only eleven.

The pain stopped only when he extracted the offending wisdom tooth. Why I let him back into my mouth after that fiasco is a mystery to me. What I learned is that handsome is as handsome does, and prestigious professional schools do not turn out uniformly smart or skilled practitioners, even in North America. Consider my ill-fated crown, for example, flung from my mouth in professional disgust by my second-to-last Canadian dentist. Obviously dentists in Canada have issues. They're not all of one mind about anyone's mouth.

The week I returned from Nicaragua, blazing smiles in all directions, CBC aired a story of an experiment in which a young woman, armed with recent x-rays and some mild dental problems, visited twenty dentists—and received twenty wildly varying estimates of work she should have done. CBC asked, not unreasonably, "Are dentists treating the patient or the insurance plan?"

I thought how delightfully different my Nicaraguan experience had been! My Nica dentist backed off from the extractions, the second implant and the bridges suggested by my last Canadian dentist. The second implant could not be done anyway, he said, because a sinus cavity was positioned too low, which would have meant a lot of pain had implant surgery gone ahead. Crowns, at a reasonable two hundred dollars each, would do the job. He even threw in the eighth crown for free.

Very quickly, I began to feel like a full partner in the adventure of reclaiming my dentition. Now this was more like it!

Naturally, the dental profession in Canada voices alarm over Canadians' voting with their air miles to visit a dentist. Note this media release from the BC Dental Association in late 2011, in which they were able to cite all of two cases of less than happy patients out of the twelve thousand per year who had received dental care in Mexico. (I haven't edited this piece except to correct punctuation and grammar errors, by the way.)

Dentistry in Mexico May Be Cheap, but Not Always Cheerful

BC Dental Association advises BC snowbirds to weigh before they pay...

British Columbians planning to winter in Arizona or California may see Mexican dental clinics as a cheaper way to meet their dental-care needs. The British Columbia Dental Association (BCDA) provides insights and recommendations to support patients in making informed dental care decisions, and encourages them to weigh the pros and cons before proceeding.

A May 25, 2011, article in The Vancouver Sun stated, "Canadians are flocking to Mexico for tooth care."

"I don't know if 12,000 Canadians represent a 'flock'," says Dr. Hank Klein, president of the BCDA, "but I do know that in 35 years, I have seen a few patients in my practice who have gone to Mexico or other countries for dental work. From what I've seen and the reports of our members, sometimes the work is fine, but when it goes wrong, it seems to go really wrong."

Mr. Robin Atchison of Vancouver would agree. "I'm 60 years old and I don't have dental insurance. Based on the experience of some friends, I did some research online and interviewed a clinic in Cancun. I went down there with two broken teeth and one cavity, which was not a big deal, but my experience was awful!

"I ended up with two caps, one on the wrong tooth, and the one with the cavity completely untouched, and a bridge over five of my upper teeth. The bridge was sitting too high in my mouth—which I tried to get them to fix while I was down there but all they would offer is to glue it in place. To make matters worse, they put the caps on without freezing—I have never been in such pain. So, now I need a lot of work to fix the mess they made of my mouth, which is going to cost me a lot more than if I had just had the original work done here from the beginning."

"Mr. Atchison's case is all too familiar to me," says Dr. Glenn van As of North Vancouver. "When you see a patient's mouth after this type of treatment, it is very disheartening for me as a clinician. It was difficult to repair the damage that had been done in Mexico to Mr. Atchison's teeth. Tremendously over prepared teeth, and a poorly fitting final restoration all meant that extensive work had to be done to try and save the teeth. It was a huge mess indeed.

"Regarding costs, I think that, fundamentally, patients in Canada are used to our public health care system that is heavily subsidized by our taxes. When they have to pay out of pocket for dental care (whether they have dental insurance or not), they are sometimes surprised by the costs.

"Dentists are surgeons who have invested seven to ten years of education after high school. We require surgical operatories in each office and professional staff who are well paid; we pay rent and business taxes in locations convenient to our patients.

"In Canada, we also use high quality materials, state-of-the-art infection-control procedures and dental labs that charge us directly for their products and services. That mix can be costly. Do we also make a good living? I hope so. I have no pension; so, after my costs, what I earn has to cover my retirement. The costs I incurred for my university training (close to $250,000 now at UBC), mandatory ongoing continuing education, setting up a practice in the Lower Mainland and living here can be prohibitively expensive. In my opinion, the fees for dental treatments are in line with the costs of delivering the care."

"I discovered in 2009 that I needed a fair bit of dental work," says Karin Janzen of Salmon Arm. "The quote seemed high on our retirement budget; so I held off. My husband and friends had dental work in Mexico and were very happy with it. The prices were remarkably less. So, in February, 2011, when a friend recommended a Mexican clinic, I decided to go to nearby Los Algodones, a border town that exists mainly for dental tourism. It was clean, professional and appeared to have all the latest high-tech equipment; so I felt I was in good hands. The dentist recommended a surprising amount of work but, since I had been neglecting things for a while, I wasn't overly surprised. The total estimate was $4,860 which included eight crowns, considerably less money than in Canada, but I proceeded with only half the work this year.

"Back home, everything seemed fine but my gums had a very sensitive spot. I went to my Canadian dentist only to discover there are multiple problems with the Mexican work. I now need a lot more expensive dental work done to repair them. What a bargain!"

"I was very concerned when Mrs. Janzen returned to our practice with an excessive amount of unnecessary work done, and of very poor quality," says Dr. Gerry Chu. "When we diagnosed her dental treatment in 2009, she needed a single crown buildup and a crown on a molar that had lost a large filling. When she returned to us in 2011, she had four crowns and three root canals—all of poor quality to the point where she may require bone grafting and implants to replace two of the teeth that were treated at the Mexican clinic."

The BCDA recognizes that dental procedures can go wrong in Canada too. BC residents can seek recourse in many ways, directly with their dentist, with the BCDA, or ultimately with a formal complaint to the College of Dental Surgeons of BC. In other countries, the oversight, complaint process and license requirements of dentists may not be the same; so recourse for problems can be vague or non-existent—especially for non-residents.

The BCDA encourages all dental patients to ask questions and create a good rapport with their dentists. "As representatives of the dentists of BC, we hope that patients will make truly informed decisions on their dental treatment—wherever they get their work done," says Dr. Klein. "We want BC dental patients to receive the highest quality care possible."

Notice that no mention is made of countries other than Mexico? Yet many Canadians visit Thailand, India, Ecuador or Nicaragua for dental work. Perhaps no complaints were forthcoming from those quarters.

Presumably the other 11,998 Canadian patients a year went back to their foreign dentists. Not a bad record.

The BCDA makes a valid point about recourse for bad dental work, should you be so unlucky. The civil law system in Nicaragua doesn't work the way Canadian and American civil courts do, and may have its decimal point a place or two over to the left when it comes to deciding what amounts would be proper compensation in a lawsuit. There's a chance you might be one of the few who fit into the same category as the two complainants from Mexico. Out of twelve thousand. There's a chance. You've been fairly warned.

Nicaragua's poverty cuts two ways. People who make only ten dollars a week cannot afford cars, books or dental services. Fortunately for Nicas, health care is free, drug costs are low, and education is free or low-cost—but they are generally unable to afford luxuries like crowns or dental implants. Like many of us in Canada, Nicaraguans often have little choice but to opt for extraction when massive tooth pain hits. Their bad luck is our good fortune in this moment in history, for, as a result of this imbalance, highly trained dentists in Nicaragua welcome patients with complex mouth problems—we represent an opportunity to use all that education fully!

Nicaragua likely has more of a certain precious commodity than today's Mexico—an earnest desire to do well by its visitors so as to get a tourist industry going. This is especially true since the financial crash of 2008, which hit the country hard. Around Leon, for example, realtors disappeared, property prices crashed, and visitor services fell on hard, hard times. Only now is the country making a comeback. The last thing any Nica wants is a dissatisfied visitor going back to North America to badmouth Nicaragua (pardon the pun!). Your dentist will strive to make you a happy customer, for the sake of his or her own practice as well as for the community and country.

Your dentist may not have the latest equipment. Dr. Baldizon's lamp had an annoying habit of going dark, but to fix it, he would have had to replace the entire chair-and-lamp assembly, an expensive proposition. So he just knocked the thing in the chops whenever it decided to turn itself off, whereupon it obediently turned itself back on. Problem solved. For now. Similarly, when he needed a panoramic x-ray of my jaws, his own little old x-ray machine couldn't do such fancy stuff; so he sent me out for that x-ray. (I paid only a few dollars for this, as I recall.) He explained that the machine was very expensive; so the Leon dentists just send patients to this single location.

Understandably: how often will local patients use this fabulous, shiny new five-thousand-dollar machine? There was no way my dentist's patients could pay him enough to buy his own machine.

Take a look at my dentist's modest but perfectly adequate set-up. All those books in the waiting room, by the way, are dental texts and notes, and they look well thumbed. Not much partying and girl-chasing went on in those student years, I'd hazard a guess.

The waiting room, with fan (the operatory is air-conditioned).

Dr. Baldizon in his air-conditioned operatory. Definitely not the opera here, but a television with subtitles and the latest programs from the US and Mexico is strategically placed to occupy the patient.

Dr. Baldizon has everything a good dentist really needs: skilled, steady hands; a capable assistant; up-to-date materials and methods; adequate equipment and a near-painless way with the needle. And television with subtitles—isn't this what you came for?

A recent US Government report, **Doing Business In Nicaragua: A Country Commercial Guide for U.S. Companies**, is very upbeat on the prospects of the dental profession there and says,

> The dental industry in Nicaragua is very well organized and highly active. Nicaraguan buyers, including specialists in periodontics, dental surgeons, and endodontics, frequently attend the Greater New York Dental Meeting (GNYDM) held in late November. There is high demand for dental implants, digital x-ray equipment, cosmetic dental supplies, disposable surgical suctioning equipment, and oral hygiene products.
>
> **Sub-Sector Best Prospects**
>
> Other best prospects related to the medical and dental sector include surgical masks and gloves, patient gratuities, other smaller utensils, and office supplies.
>
> **Opportunities**
>
> Most of the dental and most prestigious medical schools in the country, such as American University and the National Autonomous University of Nicaragua, are located in Managua and Leon. The health industry changes rapidly, therefore both dentists and doctors must actively participate in seminars and other training opportunities in order to offer their patients the most up-to-date treatments. Private healthcare workers in Nicaragua regularly participate in international trainings and seminars.
>
> The Government of Nicaragua's Ministry of Health (MINSA) regulates this industry. There is a professional Nicaraguan Dental Association, which can be reached at 505-2271-2090.

There's also a Latin American Dental Federation (FOLA), to which the Nicaraguan Odontological Federation belongs. It seems to be very busy trading professional information across South and Central America. Check it out at www.folaoral.com, where you can find contact information for the Nicaraguans under *Asociados*.

My dentist, Dr. Baldizon, took his first degree in dentistry at the National University (UNAN) which began in Leon and still has its largest campus there. He took a specialist's degree in Costa Rica and now teaches at UNAN, where he is a popular professor. He holds, in addition to his dentistry degree, a master's degree in prosthodontics and diplomas in orthodontics, orofacial pain, endodontics and periodontics.

UNAN faculty of dentistry and medicine building, Leon.

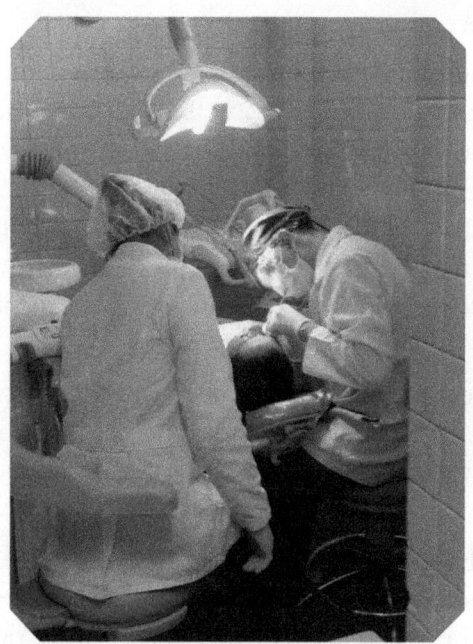

A student works on a patient, closely supervised by a practitioner like Dr. Baldizon.

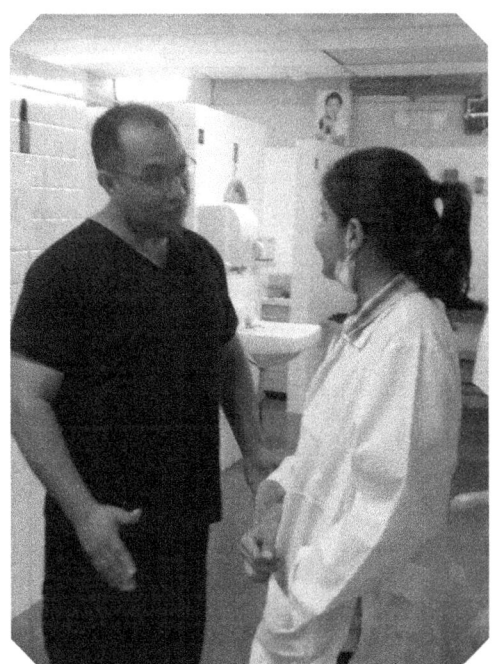

Prof. Dr. Baldizon in teaching mode.

The BCDA has a set of suggestions for dental tourists before their departure, some of which suggestions I tried to follow. Here they are (once again, edited only for English).

> **British Columbia Dental Association Recommendations for Patients to Consider** *Before* **Seeking Dental Treatment outside Canada**
>
> 1. Clearly understand what dental treatment you need *before* you leave home. Get a cost estimate from your BC dentist and a clear description of the work that is recommended – and why.
>
> 2. Compare your diagnosis and treatment plan from your BC dentist with the one you get from the dentist in the foreign country. If the foreign dentist recommends more or different work, ask why?
>
> 3. Ask your friends for referrals of foreign dentists if their *Canadian dentist* has commented that the foreign work was of good quality. Ill-fitting crowns; large connections between the teeth; or poor materials may take some time to show up as decay, inflammation, infection and pain.

4. Know your health history and how any medications you are taking may affect the dental work you want to get done. This includes knowing the names of all prescription medications you take. Make sure the foreign dentist takes your health history into consideration before proceeding.

5. Ask the foreign dentist for English copies of your dental chart notes, any x-rays, or other tests taken so that you can provide this information to your BC dentist when you return. Continuity of your dental records is important.

6. Before leaving, consult with your BC dentist to understand any post-operative complications that could arise, including infection or bleeding, and what you should do while you're away, and when you get home. Seek advice on recommended vaccinations and other things you should do to maintain your health while you're away.

7. The risk of exposure to antibiotics-resistant infectious disease is high in some countries. Check the Public Health Agency of Canada's travel website for up-to-date information.

8. Be wary of promises or claims made regarding success rates, advanced technologies, and accreditation. Good dentistry does not always come from the latest high-tech equipment.

9. *Before* you consent to the procedure, understand your recourse if things go wrong. Promises or guarantees may be meaningless for a non-resident.

10. If your decision to have dental work done in a foreign country is purely based on costs in Canada, ask your BC dentist if your recommended treatment can be staged over time, or if you can go on a payment plan to lessen the impact of the treatment costs.

11. Consider the value you place on your dental health compared to other extended health services you buy, or 'treats' you may indulge in. Budget for regular dental exams, professional cleanings and to maintain your existing fillings or other dental work so it stays in good shape. Practice good oral hygiene at home, don't smoke, and limit the sugar your teeth are exposed to each day.

Regardless of where you get your dental work done, being an active partner in your own dental care will contribute to the health, quality *and* vitality of your life as you age.

Of course, it is generally a good idea before a trip abroad to see home dentists first to get a picture of what you may need, to beef up your health and especially your immune system as much as possible, to pack along your essential medications, and to prepare to protect yourself against local problems. Beyond that, here are some comments on the points made by the BCDA.

1. I consulted three dentists before heading for Nicaragua. From the last I received a bit of a plan but no costs except more than four thousand dollars, plus tax, for each implant. Dentists don't want to be bound to fees before they have full knowledge of what's going on in one's mouth, and I don't blame them.

2. I sent my Nicaraguan dentist a list of what the Canadian dentist thought I needed, but he was not going to be bound to that list before seeing me either. He told me, however, that the cost of an implant was twelve hundred dollars and the cost of crowns two hundred dollars each. That was encouraging. As it turned out, the Canadian plan could not have been carried out, anyway.

3. My ex-pat friend was satisfied with Dr. Baldizon's work over a period of time. Getting a testimonial for work done some time ago gives you confidence. This is a good idea, if you can get it. In my case, the "ill-fitting crown, large connections between the teeth, and poor materials" all came from Canadian dentistry! I expect to be a lot happier with this Nicaraguan work and will let you know, any time you ask me on email, how my new mouth is working out.

4. Your health status and history and your medications can be sent with your initial query. It's good to be on as little medication as possible and to strengthen your immune system as much as possible before travel, which all by itself is a strain on the body.

5. Copies in English? You must be joking, BCDA! Ain't gonna happen—don't be so lazy, Canadian dentists! Get out your Spanish-English medical dictionaries (or use the bilingual vocabulary at the end of this book).

6. Fear not: your "foreign dentist" is smart enough to do this for you. If you give your home dentist another chance to scare you to death about "third-world countries", you may never get that tropical holiday *or* your dental work! No vaccinations needed for Nicaragua, by the way.

7. Water is certainly a concern in many Central American countries, but in Leon I could drink and use tap water without worry. My gastric system seems a little sensitive: I had visited Mexico five times, Guatemala twice, and Costa Rica, Dominican Republic and Nicaragua once each—and had contracted Montezuma's Revenge or something like it every trip except to the Dominican Republic. On my first trip to Nicaragua, I had stayed in a beach town for a

month and suffered through amoebic dysentery twice. The most recent trip to Nicaragua? Nothing. Couldn't have felt healthier. I attribute this to either better water or to the eight drops of black-walnut tincture in a glass of tap water I imbibed daily. The stuff kept any and all parasites at bay. (Thanks for the tip, Merri Scott!)

8. "Good dentistry does not always come from the latest high-tech equipment." Amen and Q.E.D.

9. Remember that money talks. "Practical recourse," whether you're in North or Central America, is not a lawsuit or a complaint to the governing body of the profession. Practical recourse is to pay when satisfied and not before. Start your dental work with the small stuff so that your working relationship with the dentist can get off the ground—or not. Restorations, for example, are easily re-done if necessary. In fact, in my case it did prove necessary to re-do the restorations after we whitened my teeth—and he didn't even charge me for that!

10. Notice there's no suggestion to ask your home dentist for cheaper rates!

11. I admit it—once upon a time I, Snaggletooth, wuz bad. But now I'm budgeting like a good girl—for another dental trip to Nicaragua!

How nice of the BCDA to lay out on paper its argument against dental tourism! Consider, however, that if you followed its advice Numbers 1 through 11, you would be so intimidated by your home dentists and so loaded down with paperwork, you'd never get away!

Just read this book, surf the net a little for medical tourism, Google your concerns, do the minimum you're comfortable with and fly to Nicaragua. Use your own good judgment instead of that of someone who has a vested interest in your staying put. What's the worst that could happen? The worst is this: all you get out of your trip is a cheap, interesting holiday. The best? Like me, you also lose your pain and your rotten teeth and come home with a fresh, healthy smile to go with that tan.

How Much Will It Cost?

Just as in North America, you won't be able to nail down the exact amount your dental care will cost ahead of the dentist's examination. You will have an estimate from your home dentist and a general list of things to be done, which you will send to your Nicaraguan dentist, who will respond with an estimate or a list of what he or she charges for various services. For example, a crown listed at eleven hundred dollars in North America may be listed at two hundred in Nicaragua.

I've found the Nicaraguan prices to run ten to twenty-five per cent of North American prices. Is that not amazing? It's a gift from heaven for anyone who can pull a couple of thousand dollars loose from the convoluted tangle of post-modern existence and travel there. The tropical holiday is a bonus!

I budgeted five thousand for my Nicaraguan dental work. In Canada, before tax, the two implants would have cost over nine thousand dollars; the seven crowns, seven thousand, seven hundred to over ten thousand dollars; the five restorations, another thousand; the three root canals, a couple of thousand more; the extractions, a couple of hundred; the whitening, somewhere between five hundred and eight hundred dollars; x-rays and drugs, who knows? Even if you're bad at adding frightening numbers, that tops twenty thousand dollars—without considering tax or unexpected complications, like the bone graft I needed to make the implant work.

This was the estimate I received after Dr. Baldizon's examination. It's copied exactly from the hand-written original on his letterhead. I've kept the Spanish so that you can see how easy it is to understand the dental vocabulary, since many of the words have similar forms in English. For example, the first one reads, "Seven porcelain crowns on pieces #14, 15, etc." Check the vocabulary near the end of this book if you have problems.

> 1. 7 coronas porcelana en piezas #14, 15, 18, 24, 25, 26 superior, 35 inferior. Obsequio coronas porcelana en piezas #16 y 27. Costo por Unidad U$200 x 7 = U$1,400
>
> 2. 3 Restauraciones Resina Piezas #12, 13, 23. Costo por Unidad U$20 x 3 = U$60
>
> 3. 2 Restauraciones Resina Piezas Inferiores #33, 44. Costo por Unidad U$20 x 2 = U$40

> 4. 1 Extraccion en Pieza #47 = U$10
>
> 5. Implante Dental Inferior en Pieza #47. Costo por Unidad U$1,200
>
> 6. Profilaxis = U$20
>
> 7. 3 Endodaciones. Costo por Unidad = U$250 x 3 = U$750
>
> Costo Total del Trabajo = U$3,480.00
>
> Dated: 22-09-2012   Signed: Dr. Juan Carlos Baldizon

Wow! Twenty bucks for a cleaning (*profilaxis*) or a filling, ten for an extraction, two hundred fifty for a root canal, two hundred for a porcelain crown. Most importantly, only twelve hundred for the implant.

Every time I paid some cash, a new handwritten statement would instantly show the payment and my balance. No surprises, no tax, no over-30-60-90-days calculations—just simple math, always correct. It was like stepping into a time machine back to the Fifties.

Later, once I had decided to go with the whitening treatment, there was a separate invoice for three hundred dollars—well spent! My teeth went eight shades whiter in two office sessions. I can't believe I wasted a single day dithering over that decision.

When the extraction proved difficult and time-consuming—it was that pesky molar canyon with the mini-rebars sticking up in it—there was no extra charge for the extra time needed. When I needed a bone graft to make the implant viable, there was no extra charge, either, although the material used is far from cheap. There was an eighth crown needed which the dentist threw in, I think in appreciation for the opportunity to do the entire job.

I paid for the *panoramico* x-ray and for the mouthwash and salve designed to help the bone graft take, but these were minor amounts—under twenty dollars. Dr. Baldizon's own x-rays cost nothing extra. The x-rays were helpful as they showed not only where root canals were necessary but also that the second implant recommended by the Canadian dental office could not be done because of the location of my sinuses.

How little I knew about my own face! As the root-canals painlessly drained away the prospect of those recurring, inconvenient toothaches, I realized that my face had been suffering chronic low-level pain for years. With what effects on my expression, on my smile—on my work life? I wondered. I should have done this years ago!

To think that dentures might have been all I could afford in Canada! My online research told me I would pay, at the low end of the range, twenty-nine to thirty-four hundred dollars, but it could range as high as ten thousand dollars for a set where the lower denture hooks onto implants to prevent them from popping out of one's mouth. I wondered suddenly how little that would cost in Nicaragua; so I asked Dr. Baldizon, could he provide those, too, and for how much? Yes, since he is a specialist, a prosthodontist, he certainly can, and they cost eight hundred dollars, about twenty-five per cent of the low end of the North American range.

So, if it's dentures you need, Nicaraguan ones can pay for your trip, sightseeing trips included.

How Do I Plan My Trip?

How Long Should I Plan to Stay?

The quick answer? As long as you can afford to be away.

The longer answer? It depends.

First, ask your dentist how long he or she thinks it will take to accomplish the work list you sent. Then double it. Why? Stuff happens. Besides, you want to plug in some beach time and maybe some time to wander around the country and feel good about how much fun you're having on so little money.

In my case, Dr. Baldizon estimated two weeks. So I planned for a month. It was perfect. Sure enough, stuff happened. I needed time to think about the tooth-whitening. I needed time to explore Granada and the mountains. Making contacts for my business and professional concerns took time. I was supposed to write a book between dental sessions (that one didn't happen, but at least I planned for it). The technician building my crowns needed five days. A truck hit me and I needed a day or two to come back to myself.

A month was perfect. It was long enough that I didn't resent the time it always takes to sort oneself out and get settled into new surroundings, nor the time it takes to recover from or prepare for a long day of air travel. Most items on my list were satisfactorily crossed off. I felt relaxed, and healthier by the day (except for the bit with the truck—more about that later).

Figure out how much time the dentist needs, and what you, personally, would like to do while you're in Nicaragua. Then buy trips on Tuesdays through Thursdays, which, I understand, are usually the cheapest flights.

Some dental sagas will take more than one visit. Mine, for example, requires a nine-month wait after the bone graft, to be sure it has taken. Then the implant can be completed.

Dear me! Another trip to Nicaragua—what a hardship!

Next trip, I will make time for a return to the island of Ometepe and more exploration of this beautiful country. Would you care to come along?

Where Should I Stay?

One of your cheapest and best options is a home-stay as part of enrolling in a Spanish school (see "Enroll in a Spanish School"). You can't beat two hundred to two hundred-fifty dollars for twenty hours' tuition, including room and board for a week.

However, home-stay and school five half-days a week tie you down to a schedule which might be difficult to mesh with the dental schedule. Fear not: there are lots of other options, all of them bargains in the light of North American prices.

For the young at heart, hostels are an excellent option, with accommodations ranging from dormitories to private rooms with baths for very little money—seven dollars a night is not uncommon. Aside from meeting travelers from all over the world—and probably someone from your own home town—you will enjoy the kitchen privileges which give you control over your food budget and preferences, and the ubiquitous online access. Our hostel in Granada, the Oasis, not only offers varied accommodation, lots of wi-fi, breakfast service, free Continental breakfast (not my cup of tea, personally, but it's there for those who like it), advice, and trips to everywhere near Granada, but also boasts a lovely swimming pool and aesthetically pleasing courtyards and hallways—all included in the price: twenty-five dollars for two in a private room with bath. Hostels, however, often lack elevators and never have bathtubs, only showers (as far as I know). The lights-out or quiet-time rules, which vary from hostel to hostel, might bother night owls.

Leon has many great hostels (*hostales*). Try Bigfoot Hostel, Via Via Hostel, Sonati Hostel, El Albergue, Casa Vieja, Monkey Republic, Colibri, La Siesta Perdida ("lost sleep"—odd name!), Tortuga Boluda, La Clinica, Don Raul, Casa Iguana or Hostal San Sebastian. They are all quite centrally located and most have an online presence.

Hotels charge less than their counterparts in North America. The Best Western in Leon cited forty-eight dollars per night—but they still don't offer bathtubs, only showers. Chain hotels are few and far between, but one can find fine local hotels. Five blocks from my dentist stands the recently re-opened Los Balcones, a very attractive colonial hotel with moderate prices and a pleasant restaurant and bar (no doubt they'll expand their wine list from two bottles to half a dozen by the time I return). Il Convento is the one everyone in Leon will steer you to, as the city's number-one historic and classy hotel. Enjoy the art in the halls around the restaurant. Consult an up-to-date travel guide, or their website, however, before taking the financial plunge here.

There's a growing group of private accommodations which might best be labeled bed-and-breakfasts. Great old colonial houses are being turned into guest accommodations by ex-pats, catering especially to the frequent or long-term visitor. You won't find their information on travel-brochure stands; these inexpensive niches fill up by word of mouth. (Email me if this is your preference.)

One place that defies labeling is the long-term accommodation behind Pan y Paz Panaderia (Bread and Peace Bakery), with chocolate croissants to die for, superbly healthy lunches and lots of room and wi-fi to work on your computer all day if it pleases you. Run by a darling dog whose humans are French and Dutch, the Pan y Paz is never short of customers. You'll be hooked the first time you try it.

I've saved the best for last. El Nancite is a cross between a hostel and a hotel. Owner John Coronna built it by hand with a wonderful sense of space, color, and light, the building punctuated by two courtyards full of organically grown fruit and ornamental trees. As many as two dozen guests could fill this hotel, only six blocks from my dentist, although many nights I was virtually the only guest. My private room with bath cost twenty-five dollars per night, complete with cable TV and wi-fi.

El Nancite was peaceful, quiet and cool, and other guests were invariably interesting people. John, a New Yorker with a Nica family and a strong philanthropic bent, is absorbed in the youth projects he works on all day, letting family members run the hotel. Every morning, however, no later than seven, John arrived at the hotel to cook breakfast from scratch for his guests, even if I was the only one. As I munched on crepes or eggs cooked to match the changing needs of my dentition, we talked philosophy, philanthropy and the state of the world. Those weren't three-dollar breakfasts—they were gold-plate breakfasts, the kind of travel encounter you never forget.

Perhaps needless to say, John's hotel received the maximum number of stars in my Trip Advisor review of El Nancite. On my return next year, without question this hotel will be my home base. Coming along? Take a look at these pictures and consider whether you'd pay twenty-five dollars a night to stay here.

A welcoming smile in the lobby.

Enjoy breakfast and philosophy here.

Quiet dining space.

Second courtyard, with organic plantings.

Lovely room with own stairs.

My window.

Should I Rent a Car?

No. With taxis charging only twenty cords (under a dollar) to take you pretty well anywhere in town, and *taxistas* charging you very little more than the gas for taking you anywhere in the country and acting as guide as well, why would you?

Anyway, safe parking is hard to find. Cars and their accessories are expensive commodities, inviting theft and pillage. City car-owners park their cars *inside* the house.

The funniest—and initially most puzzling—signage in Nicaragua is the proliferation of the garage-sale signs familiar to anyone living in North America. You know the ones: plastic, eighteen-by-twenty-four-inch white signs with red and black printing stating, "Garage Sale" with a space below to write in the address and/or date of the sale. *Why would people bring these things back from the US or Canada,* I quizzed myself, *only to write in "CARRO" instead of the specifics of the sale?* It made no sense, especially since I never saw a single garage sale in Nicaragua. I have no idea how people pass on unwanted stuff in Nicaragua, but it certainly isn't by garage sale. Perhaps there was some location called *Carro* where people gathered for a flea market?

Finally it dawned on me. The word for *garage*, in Spanish, is spelled exactly as in English, although the pronunciation is quite different (gah-rah-ghay). Second, there is a Spanish word spelled *sale* which means *he, she, or it leaves* (sah-lay). Third, in Spanish syntax, the subject often comes after the verb rather than before. So *Garage: sale carro* means, *Look out, cars emerging from the garage here.*

No, don't get a car unless you're a masochist or going to be in Nicaragua for a long time. Aside from parking woes and signage misunderstandings, there are far too many interesting things going on along the roadways and streets, like one-ways, cows, burro carts, chicken buses and a certain percentage of reckless drivers, for a person to pay attention to when one's mouth is being seriously worked on.

Take a chicken bus if you're into adventure. Take a taxi if not.

What about Insurance?

Travel insurance, that is. By all means take the top insurance, from loss of baggage to medical. There is no downside except cost and you cannot know what will happen, wherever you are in the world. The nice part about travel is, you will be insured against the slings and arrows of outrageous fortune even if you weren't insured at home. For a month, mine cost about two hundred sixty dollars.

When I was hit by the truck, I was lucky—no major injury. My treatment at the Nica hospital was free. Had I died, however, the insurance would have seen to it that my remains were flown home. Had I required surgery, I would likely have opted to be flown home for it.

It's just good sense to buy good travel insurance.

What Should I Pack?

Medicine: take along your necessary medicines, enough of them to last through the whole trip if they are uncommon. Common medicines and non-prescription remedies are available in the zillion *farmacias* at incredibly lower prices than in North America. For example, the dental mouthwash and salve I needed is far more easily come by in Nicaragua than in Canada, at about an eighth of the price.

Clothes: take cotton, linen or rayon only. Silk, wool, leather, polyester, acrylic—they're all too hot for us temperate-zone creatures unless they're bathing suits. Temperatures in Leon can exceed ninety degrees Fahrenheit, to the point where you really look forward to an afternoon rainstorm or an air-conditioned movie or shopping stop. If you're deconditioned, overweight or menopausal, this is especially true.

You will be most comfortable in loose-fitting clothing—leave the leggings-below-cute-cleavage style to the lovely young lady Nicas who grew up with the heat. Don't bother taking a coat—you'll live through the cold of the airports and you certainly don't need a coat anywhere in Nicaragua. If you are going into the mountains of Nicaragua or into the cloud forests, a light sweater or unlined cotton jacket will feel good but in the unlikely event you need anything more, somebody will give you a blanket.

For sleep, I recommend a pure cotton or rayon single garment that fits loosely, like a sundress—something without the fire-retardant and chemicals that can turn bedclothes into heat sinks. In your hotel, insist on cotton sheets; they breathe. (I was miserable on the polyester-clad slabs in a hotel in Matagalpa.) Good sleep is essential to a happy time in your dentist's office—be sure you have a competent shower, and sheets and PJs that breathe through the night with you.

I had four sundresses and wore them in rotation. I wore the incredibly light sweater to the air-conditioned movies the first time but didn't need it. The cotton pocket capris? Once. The shorts and tops? Not at all.

Don't bring laundry supplies, irons or steamers. Send out your laundry through the hotel, or swish it in the sink and hang it up in the bath.

This is what the packing experts say, "Pack. Then repack, throwing half of it out." I thought I'd done that but I should have done it twice.

Remember that the arty things worth carrying back from Nicaragua, soapstone carvings and pottery, are not light. Go with a half-empty suitcase if you like that kind of stuff.

On my trip to the cloud forest, I did appreciate a light sweater for part of one day. On my trip to Jinotega in the mountains, two layers of light cotton proved perfect.

As for shoes, remember those sidewalk pictures? Go for surefootedness, comfort and durability. If your feet are big, you may not find too many shoes in your size. As a size nine or nine and a half, I took along four pair of lightweight footwear; one pair broke but, to my surprise, I found a couple of pair of lovely women's sandals at astonishingly good prices and came home with five sets of footwear! For women who aren't Bigfoot's relatives (like my poor daughter, with size 13 feet), Nicaragua is a shoe-lover's paradise, but stick to the stores rather than the market kiosks if you value quality. Or so I was told.

Books: Since the advent of e-readers, people don't need to carry along a library. However, a beautiful book is still a prized and expensive item and makes a great gift for your hosts. If you prefer, as do my aging eyes, to read your fiction in an actual book, there are hostels and travel outfits only too glad to pass on your read books and let you take away a fresh one. So, by all means take along a lightweight book or two with the intention of trading it for another somewhere along your travels.

Electronics: Take your e-book reader, your tablet or laptop, and your favorite camera. The country is wired. As said before, get a local phone if you're not interested in paying roaming charges.

Supplements: I'm perhaps seen as a bit of a nut on natural supplements, although they've saved me from early termination of this carbon unit over and over. So, here is what I learned about buying supplements in Nicaragua: like anything else, they are comfortingly inexpensive—if you can find them. But I did. After asking around for hawthorn for my heart in every *farmacia* for three weeks (*Tiene Usted espino blanco? Majuelo? Para el corazon?*), I suddenly found a hole-in-the-wall pharmacy dedicated to natural medicine and there the stuff was, although apparently not native to Nicaragua. Cheaper, even, than at home.

My favorite cheap medicine, baking soda, was a surprisingly different story. I assumed, knowing that the big grocery stores, La Union and Paly, are Walmart-owned, that baking soda in the familiar orange boxes would grace the shelves of every grocery—not! Even the shelves with flour and baking powder did not show any baking soda. "Oh, they're just out of it," locals assured me. Well, if so, they were "out" for my entire month there. Meanwhile, my ex-pat friend who bakes wonderful bread took me to the *tienda* of baking supplies, where, sure enough, baking soda was trotted out in half-pound plastic baggies secured with those awful metal ties. I bought ten; I like baking soda. I use it for de-tox baths, mouth cleansing, skin treatment and alkalinization. Happily I poured out a baggie into the floor of my huge shower for a nice soak, only to find that this white stuff seemed to have less oomph than the stuff in the familiar orange boxes at home. I made and remade this observation through all the ten baggies as I piled it onto my toothbrush and poured a solution of it over myself in the shower. It just didn't seem to have what it takes. Maybe it was cut with corn starch? Who knows? It didn't even fulfill my expectations as a cleaning solution.

Next time, I'm packing along a couple of kilos of baking soda. The real stuff. In the orange boxes.

If you take a certain supplement every day and would miss it, bring enough of it along. I can't tell you about the availability of colloidal silver, red-reishi mushrooms, or thyroid supplements because I brought enough of that stuff along in my suitcase. I suggest you do the same with your can't-do-withouts. Remember the rule about carrying liquids and goop on board and put your month's supply into the checked baggage.

Foods: It's time to tell you bad news: it's safer not to eat or drink during your flight. Radiation at the altitudes jets use is high nowadays. Up to twenty thousand feet or so, there's no problem, but above that, ionizing radiation as measured by my radiation monitor is well into the red danger zone since the Fukushima accident. It gets better as you fly south, beyond the jetstream: the radiation thirty-seven thousand feet above Nicaragua measures only two thirds of what it is over the US and Canada. For maximum health, it seems prudent to avoid eating or drinking anything that may have been on a large plane for any length of time. Eat and drink before you take off, or after, and don't pack along any unnecessary food.

I use my radiation monitor for peace of mind about what to eat. I took along some of my favorite chocolate to Nicaragua and it measured out fine upon landing. On a previous trip (to Colorado), however, I had taken along salmon but upon landing it measured rather close to the high-radiation line. At this time it seems that some foods, the ones usually low in radiation to start with, weather a plane trip without a problem, while some sensitive items like fish take on extra radiation.

Let me encourage you to leave food behind and instead enjoy the fresh food in Nicaragua, which measures out totally normal, much lower, even, than does produce in North America.

If by now you are suspecting I am a nutcase, be assured you are not alone. But I'm not alone, either, out there with my little radiation monitor. I'm in good scientific company when I disclose to you that ionizing radiation from Japan is an ongoing phenomenon which currently affects mostly the jetstream, 'way up there where the big planes fly. The radioactive iodine we were worried about in the first few months after the nuclear accident at Fukushima is all gone now, as its half life was eight days. However, there is concern over the eighty or more other radioactive compounds wafting across the northern hemisphere, which are capable of coming down pretty well anywhere it decides to rain. The extra great news about visiting Nicaragua is that so far Central America is fairly free of such radiation and the produce there measures out at normal background levels.

Don't bring food: you don't need it. Many foods are cheaper in Nicaragua, anyway. Local produce like bananas, pineapples and veggies are dirt cheap. Grass-fed beef is three dollars a pound. Imported cheese is dear but local cheese is an incredible bargain. Even very drinkable wines, mostly imported from South America, cost six dollars per bottle where in Canada, even on sale, one forks over a tenspot. You would really, really have to try to eat yourself broke in Nicaragua.

Children and pets: Nicas are family-oriented and always ask after one's children. I haven't any doubt that small children traveling with you would be quickly spoiled rotten with loving attention and you'd have no problem finding baby sitters while you're at the dentist.

Dogs? Not so much, although Nica dogs, always nearly hairless until you get up into the mountains where the air is fresh and cool, are also obviously well loved. There's no sign of a dog-care industry. There may be one but if so, it's in hiding.

Cats? You're kidding, right? Nicaragua has enough cats. I'm told their lives are nasty, brutish and short. Besides, there are really big ones in the jungle... like jaguars and pumas. Leave Puss at home.

My friend Julia has enough felines without rescuing yours!
Hmm...what happened to the other thirteen?

Mouth and Body Prep

Both travel and extensive dental work take it out of you. A new environment, however pleasant, tests your immune system and the loving attentions of a dentist can tire you out. Besides, travel isn't fun anymore—that old, old airline slogan, "Half the fun is getting there," sounds ironic nowadays. Then there's the phenomenon known as the "relaxation response": you finally get a chance to relax on vacation from the stress of you work environment and—wouldn't you know it? You get a cold or the flu, first thing. Rats!

It doesn't have to be that way. I felt so healthy on this dental vacation, I was amazed. On previous vacations, I've fallen prey to gastro-intestinal illness or a recurrence of my chronic problems, like fibromyalgia. This time? *Nada*. Other than the mechanical effects of being hit by the truck, my body suffered no ill effects at all. It bounced back from the jaw surgery and even healed up the wounds from the truck incident in a week. How did that happen?

I attribute my stronger immune system to the boning up and beefing up during the previous several months. A cancer survivor, I'd studied up on how to avoid contracting the big C again by using natural medicine. Only time will tell how successful that effort is but meanwhile I can report to you, my readers, that strengthening my immune system by these methods has worked very well to help the body endure treatment as well as sudden changes in environment—like medical or dental tourism. This is not medical advice, obviously. It's just what works for the body I have to live in, and it may work for you, too.

The gist of these methods is to de-acidify the body. You want to put out the fires of inflammation throughout the body (any condition whose name ends in the syllables *itis* is an inflammatory condition) and you want to kill off any fungus on your skin or inside you. In particular, you want to prepare your mouth by getting rid of plaque and gingivitis as much as possible before the invasive dental work begins. As many cancer patients know, that means that alkalinizing the body is crucial to healing and wellbeing. I am proof that even incomplete alkalinization can make enormous differences in your response to treatment.

So here's what I did before the plane took off for Nicaragua.

I taught myself to sleep seven to nine hours a night.

I used baking soda to brush my teeth and made sure I ingested half a teaspoon of the stuff a day—even grew to like the salty taste. I used Lugol's Solution to ensure my tired old thyroid was getting enough iodine and the body was getting its iodide. A magnesium-chloride spray or gel eased sore or swollen spots. I never go anywhere anymore without enough supplies of these three guardian-angel substances to tide me over the trip.

I put my pedometer back on and let the dog encourage me to walk ten thousand steps a day.

I switched to green tea with stevia in the morning, instead of my beloved espresso coffee. Don't ask me how this happened—the body just decided one day. Now it lets me have perhaps one or two cappuccinos a week. Much as I hate to admit it, I feel better, my saliva tastes fresher, and I don't stain my teeth with coffee. Darn it! I miss the *idea* of having good coffee!

I dropped baked goods other than sprouted-grain bread. I tried to minimize red meat, alcohol, gluten and glucose and eat only home-cooked and home-grown stuff. Coconut oil became my goop of choice both for cooking and for treating the skin. Baking soda became my bath salts as well as my favorite cleanser for the kitchen and bath.

Using hours of research plus the trial-and-error method, I put together a suite of supplements that works for me. These include hawthorn, red-reishi mushroom, zinc, selenium, glutathione, vitamins C and D3, and an oriental concoction entertainingly named Free and Easy Wanderer. To do this, I not only spent days online but also consulted two allopathic (regular) doctors, an Ayurvedic doctor and a Chinese medicine specialist. I leave it to your imagination how different the prescriptions of the allopathic doctors were from the suggestions of the natural medicine practitioners.

Today I am not on any prescription medications and I feel younger and stronger than I have in twenty years. After the trip I realized that I had not been successful in putting out all the inflammation in my face, only in banking those fires—draining those root canals finished off the pain, what a relief! I also realize now that it doesn't take much to encourage new inflammation to flare up elsewhere in the body—this is going to be a life-long battle. At least, however, now I don't feel helpless against these flames. These tools give me a measure of control over the body which I never enjoyed before. You can have this control, too.

Since my dental treatment in Nicaragua, I've done research on how to prevent plaque and gingivitis naturally. This came about because the chlorhexadine-containing mouthwash that was so cheap and easy to procure in Nicaragua proved elusive, weaker and more expensive in Canada. (Plus, you have to have a prescription for it. Good luck finding a dentist at home who is willing to give you a prescription after you bought all your treatment elsewhere!)

The first tool in controlling plaque and gingivitis is figuring out who the bad guys are. That was easy: sucrose, glucose, fructose, lactose, and maltose, which interact with detrimental bacteria to form lactic acid and glue themselves to the teeth with the help of dextran. Take a magnifying glass to the grocery store next time you shop, to read ingredient lists of your favorite foods, and you will begin to wonder if modern foods are *designed* to create tooth plaque and support the toothpaste industry or the dental profession!

I suspected there might be natural alternatives to chlorhexadine, which, while killing off the streptococcus bacteria whose only joy in life is the creation of plaque, has a disadvantage. Potentially, it can form calculus (tartar, not the mathematical kind) on the teeth or even stain your pearly whites.

Sure enough, there are alternatives, all of them more easily obtained than chlorhexadine. Here is the list of natural substances I found which are said to inhibit the formation of plaque and gingivitis. All of us might as well make a habit of using these, starting now.

- Bloodroot (Indian paint; *sanguinaria canadensis*): I'm familiar with the plant from my prairie childhood—never knew it tasted so…rough.
- Green tea and stevia: my favorite way to drink green tea!
- The tannins found in coffee and tea (but they may stain teeth).

- Zinc.
- Pycnogenol (as an ingredient of chewing gum).
- Propolis (in toothpaste or mouthwash).
- Cherry juice. Yum.
- Mastic (as an ingredient of chewing gum).
- Oil of oregano (also good for killing a toothache). It's an acquired taste.
- Retanhia root—this stuff is the bomb. Made by Weleda, it comes in small, ten-dollar-ish bottles that last a long time, as you simply add five to ten drops to a little warm water for a delicious, freshening mouthwash—even my dog likes it. Weleda makes a toothpaste with retanhia, too.

Start re-mastering your mouth and your body today. Every step you take, however small, will improve your dental experience, your travels, and your life. Why wait for spring?

What Else Can I Do While in Nicaragua?

Trips and R&R
In Leon

Leon's streets and markets host not only a lot of the city's small business but much of its social life. Every few blocks, a park or square offers you opportunities just to sit on a bench and indulge in people-watching. On the main square—if its renovations are ever finished—you can park yourself in a café with a cup of tea or Nicaraguan coffee or beer and watch the world go by.

Shopping is much more of an adventure in Nicaragua than in North America. If you collect art or craftwork, there's a lot of prowling around involved before you flush out your quarry. My first visit, I found only one art gallery, hiding in a lawyer's office. I bought four good paintings there, ranging from sixty to three hundred dollars. Second trip, I found another gallery and a good artist who has his own studio. Both visits, I bought sculpture and pottery at Kaman, a store (located kitty-corner across the main square from the El Sesteo restaurant) which carries a fairly representative collection of Nicaraguan sculpture, pottery and jewelry.

Irresistible pottery with an irresistible seller, himself a potter.

Foodies always have fun in a new country, starting their hunt in the local grocery store and sniffing out what's truly local before venturing into the wilds of the market. Aside from local veggies, meats and cheese, air-conditioned La Union carries local teas and coffees, jams, sauces, bitters, rum, some chocolate and even, to my delight since I can't get it in Canada, powdered whole milk. (I took a huge can of the stuff back home in that half-empty large suitcase.)

I stopped at La Union pretty well every day I was in Leon, partly for the break from the heat, partly for the mango ice cream, partly to see what was new. You don't want to use the ATM there because the withdrawal limit is very low, about thirty dollars (for which your bank will charge you a five-dollar fee) but the ice-cream stand right next to it is a bargain. It doesn't hurt that the four-screen movie palace is right next door, offering a delightfully cool siesta substitute for a hot afternoon, at only four dollars for newly released films with subtitles. A cool way to study Spanish!

Booklovers will love to browse the University's bookstore, whose stock is almost all Spanish but includes children's books you can bring home as gifts for young learners—or for yourself. Novels in English, French or German are found on book-trading shelves for pennies—or free—in hotels, hostels and touring companies.

There is nightlife in Leon, although by ten o'clock the city is certainly quieter than an average North American city of similar size. There's an early-evening bustle of business that shuts down by ten, and little restaurants devoted entirely to the provision of meals generally close down about that time, too. The movies, cafes, student hangouts and nightclubs carry on until late hours. I'm told there's even a casino or two in Leon, although I didn't come across them.

Near Leon

From Leon, the easiest, cheapest day trip is by local bus from El Mercadito, for twelve cords (fifty cents), down to Poneloya and Las Penitas, two beach towns that melt into each other. (A taxi takes only fifteen minutes and two hundred fifty cords, about eleven dollars, but you won't get to see both places on one taxi trip.) In two to three hours, you can walk from the far end of Poneloya to the other end of Las Penitas, on the beach one way and on the street the other, if you are so inclined.

You'll want to rest your weary feet at the end of Las Penitas, at the Hostal Barco de Oro or one of its neighbors, close to the Isla Juan Venado. Here you'll enjoy a local beer or a decent glass of wine and wonder why on earth you haven't planned for more time on this spectacular beach. Perhaps you'll cough up seven dollars to stay the night so that you can take a morning trip by boat through the mangrove swamp to see the alligators of Isla Juan Venado.

The beach fronting Barco do Oro seems to go on forever.

Walk back up the street to pick up the bus after a great meal and superb coffee at the Tsunami Taco Bar, where Canadian owner Taco Dave will regale you with tales of what life is really like for ex-pats on the beach.

Canadian, eh?

Across from Hotel Playa Roca on Las Penitas' fabulous beach, Taco Dave's Tsunami Bar is a great place to catch the bus—or let another bus sail by to do full justice to the coffee 'n' conversation.

A second must-see day trip takes you to Leon Viejo, the old location of Leon, which the Spaniards abandoned only ninety years after its founding because of volcanic activity. Even if you don't like history, you'll love this serene, lovely place. You may want a guide to help with the Spanish and round out the stories of what happened here three centuries ago—it's a wild story, complete with murder, betrayal and sexual afflictions. This tour is often combined with a volcano tour; so ask around at the tour shops like Via Via, Bigfoot, Tierra Tours, Green Pathways and Quetzal Trekkers.

A popular day trip from Leon involves climbing a dormant volcano, El Cerro Negro (it's sleeping pretty lightly, if you ask me), and then either riding a board down its precipitous slope or "walking" down the "trail". Volcano boarding takes only a few minutes to reach the bottom but the alternative takes as long as it takes you to gather up your courage—plus an hour or so. If you have balance problems or unreliable knees, hips or feet, take my advice and your camera: stay at the base of the volcano and enjoy watching the human mountain goats have their fun. Put your bathing suit on and tan those stubborn legs until it's time to go for a swim in the volcanic lagoon nearby.

On top of Old Smoky. "Tell me again how to get off this thing? You must be joking!"

Beyond Leon

Day trips and longer, involving walking, hiking, kayaking, fishing, surfing and horseback riding, are arranged by companies like Green Pathways, who also offer tours of Leon. These trips are a great way to access the volcano chain, Isla Juan Venado, coffee and chocolate farms, the mountains and the cloud forests, one to three days at a time. You have a guide who speaks your language as well as Spanish and you build unforgettable camaraderie with the other travelers in your group.

Longer trips, to Granada, Ometepe, or San Juan del Sur, you can handle yourself. Make an online reservation for your first night's accommodation, for example, and then travel by a combination of chicken bus and taxi to the destination area. From there, take local guided trips and explore on your own. (Take only a small bag to make bus travel easier!)

I haven't yet visited popular San Juan del Sur but I can unload tips on visiting Granada and Ometepe, the island that should make the list of One Hundred Places to See before You Die. If there's an official list of OHP2Sb4YD, it doubtless includes elegant Granada, but fewer people know the delights of Ometepe, which surely is the original Land of Smiles.

To reach Ometepe, travel to San Jorge, the boat-launch town. That's not a one-step operation by bus, and traveling by bus with anything more than a grocery-bag's equivalent of luggage is difficult; so you may want to opt for a taxi from Leon to San Jorge, which will cost you just over one hundred dollars—it's a long ride. Or you can spend about ten dollars by going to the Leon bus station, catching a bus to Managua and there switching to a bus for San Jorge before getting a cab ride to the dock.

Early arrival at the dock is a good idea. Lago Nicaragua and Ometepe are so big that they make their own weather, which means the afternoon can be a wild, sloshy ride in the launch. Check the ferry schedule before you leave Leon to be sure to get on. Our launch left San Jorge before three p.m. and arrived on the island two and a half hours later. We were well sloshed by then and not in the preferred way! By contrast, our return to San Jorge, on the island's so called big ferry at eight in the morning, was a serene and comfortable trip over calm waters.

You will hear that there is a ferry from Granada to Ometepe. *How convenient*, you think. Not! It leaves Granada—infrequently—in the dark and arrives about four in the morning; I gather it's mostly for commercial shipping.

Once you offload, a flock of *taxistas* will descend upon you. Yes, you will pay what seems like a steep taxi fare—twenty-five dollars to our hotel, El Encanto. Don't worry; it's worth it.

I recommend El Encanto for its cleanliness, beauty and serenity for its restaurant, its gardens, and its proprietor, Juan Carlos Espino, originally from El Salvador, and his family (including two sweet, well mannered dogs). The only problem with staying here forever, to write book after book, perhaps, is the lack of online access. Wi-fi can still be iffy on Ometepe. So, I was incommunicado—that was a real holiday! On the other hand, I'll be glad for El Encanto's sake as well as mine if Juan Carlos has ensured stable online access by my next visit.

One day—that's all the time I had to explore wonderful Ometepe. Here are some pictures to encourage you to plan for more time on this island which reminds me so much of Maui, Hawaii, in its vegetation, its two-volcanoes-joined-by-an-isthmus configuration, and its sensibility—Maui as it could have been, might have been. As I wish it could be: no shopping malls, no acres of pavement, no frippery of civilization—just beaches, small towns and farms, gorgeous greenery and flora, and forty-three thousand people who can't stop smiling.

The view from Finca Magdalena, once a farm of the Somoza family.

Bolivar points to the date at the end of the calendar—2012!

The freshwater beach. There aren't too many of those on the planet.

Ancient Nahuatl statues of guardians and deities, protected by the Church.

Three-dimensional map of Ometepe in the central park of Altagracia.

A few words and pictures about Granada, because I know you want to go there, if only to be sure that you made the right choice in opting for Leon.

Take the carriage ride from the central park to see this lovely city the fast and easy way. The drivers are great guides.

Horse-drawn carriages lined up at the central park.

Statue honoring mothers.

Family life on a Sunday afternoon.

Have the most indulgent breakfast of your life at the Choco Museo's full-breakfast buffet, which fronts the Hotel Spa Granada, a place full of surprises. Not only will you be waylaid by the fascinating museum of chocolate—and perhaps hang around for a chocolate-making class—but as your artistic sensibilities draw you back through the spacious halls hung with original paintings and beautifully staged with suites of art furniture, you come upon the resort at the rear of the property—pool, bar, spa and sunshine. The works. Much as I appreciated the Oasis hostel, this hotel is where you'll find me next time, on one of those deck chairs, reading a real book and eating real chocolate as I work extra hard on the eternal task of tanning one's ancient legs.

The resort hiding at the rear of Hotel Spa Granada.

Now for something completely different: Jinotega, a mountainous province neighboring Leon. If you have a yen for the Wild West, cowboys, horses, forests and fresh mountain air, this is the trip for you, unveiling an unexpected face of Nicaragua quite unlike the beach-bunny and awesome-colonial-history pictures the tourism industry urges upon you. I went via the city of Matagalpa, which I did not like much, through Selva Negra (the black forest, so named by German settlers) and on to Jinotega, a clean, open, fun-loving town that seems quirky, isolated, but honest about what it is.

Lagoon at Selva Negra

Painting of the old days in the mountains.

There are plenty of trips I could recommend besides these, but then this would be a book more about travel in Nicaragua than about fixing your teeth. Suffice it to say that in Nicaragua there's something for every traveler. You won't be bored between your sessions in the dental chair.

Business or Research

As a North American traveler, you bring with you to Nicaragua a set of skills and assets few Nicas can equal. Don't be surprised if, during your trip, ideas come to you for enhancing your business while stimulating Nicaragua's economy.

Working in Nicaragua is necessarily a labor of love, as wages are so very low. My Canadian friend who teaches English at the University calculates he makes about ten dollars per evening—if he doesn't spend it on gas to get there or on taking his students out for coffee. I was asked to bring an English course to Ometepe—an exciting idea! I asked what the speaker thought people could afford to pay for such a course. Twenty dollars, was the answer. I wasn't discouraged. Who knows what wonderful things might come out of holding such a course?

It only makes sense that, if you can live well in Nicaragua on seven hundred dollars per month, there won't be many jobs that offer more than that.

As an educator, writer and publisher, I tripped over a surprising number of business ideas, contacts and opportunities. Naturally, I'm always doing research for the next novel and Nicaragua is a treasure trove of material for that. Nicaragua is also hungry for my chief products, good English and independent publishing. In Nicaragua, the former is rare and the latter, apparently non-existent. Doubtless the University needs to localize its publishing. I can imagine working with Nica educators to install a super ESL course for youth, while Granada looks like a good town to hold Spanish-in-Three-Days courses for travelers and ex-pats.

Whatever is nearest and dearest to you can form a good excuse for future trips to Nicaragua and beyond. As it is written, do what you love and the money will follow. In Nicaragua's case, probably not much money will follow, but at least you can legitimately write off your trip as a business expense.

On the material side, I have an organic agricultural product viable for Nica farmers and gardeners. This opened the door to contact with people I would never have met had I not brought samples and information along.

You, too, may have a product that would prosper in Nicaragua. Check with the airlines before packing your samples, however, and remember that the US will ask you to declare business materials as well as plant and animal matter even if you are merely passing through that country.

Learning

We have already spoken of the many Spanish schools in Nicaragua, most of which offer you a wide choice, from a single lesson at a time to full days with a private tutor. The group classes usually include field trips, which necessarily involves further learning—have fun!

Private organizations like the Choco Museo in Granada offer courses in what they do best, like chocolate-making. (Can you tell this is high on my list for my next visit?) The tour companies know where these brief courses are and often offer them as part of a trip. I've seen courses in local cuisine, permaculture, dance, and traditional crafts. Too bad life is so short!

Volunteer

I've been told that every year dentists from all over Nicaragua and the world descend on Managua for a couple of weeks to offer low-cost or no-cost dentistry to Nicas who could not otherwise afford a dentist. I've heard of vets offering free neutering clinics. I've tutored several people in the tourist business to a better accent in English, and am chewing on the idea of bringing down a group of Canadian kids to work on a youth project with their Nica counterparts.

If you are in Nicaragua for any significant length of time, you are bound to meet people involved with the many community-service organizations there. Listen for the sound of a door opening. You also may have a gift of skill, knowledge or lovingkindness to pass on in Nicaragua.

What Should I Watch Out For?

Trucks!

Yes, I was struck by a truck. As a pedestrian. In an intersection. By a truck considerably bigger than a pick-up.

Pedestrians do not, apparently, enjoy right of way on Nicaragua's streets. I was crossing near the rear of a pack of pedestrians, all of whom must have been nimbler than I, when the truck waiting to make a turn into our street suddenly did so. Bullseye! The driver hit me dead center (pardon the pun). I'll never forget the sound of the truck thwacking my left side, the side from which I had always thought death would come. Down I went, with time for a single thought: *This is it. This is the last minute of living.*

I came to, lying on the cobblestones, the truck tires millimeters from my body and the license plate right above my face. I must have been in shock; I was dimly aware of many kind hands moving my body away from the truck. Somehow I was bundled into a taxi and driven to a hospital, where a saline was jabbed into my arm along with something for shock and pain and I was wheeled swiftly into an x-ray room.

Aside from being covered in dirt on my right side, a gash on the shoulder, a huge lump on the head and a broken tooth that had pierced my cheek just above the lip, I seemed to have survived pretty well. Concern over a possible concussion kept me in the hospital for a while and encouraged me to sleep sitting up for a couple of nights, but my main worry was whether the impact had damaged my dental work! My first thought on seeing the cheek wound was, *Thank goodness Dr. Baldizon hasn't fixed that one yet!*

Other than a missed appointment, the accident didn't affect the dental work, but it certainly affected how I cross the streets! Traffic lights and zebra crossings are extinct species as far as Leon is concerned; so being a law-abiding pedestrian doesn't make any difference—the laws are different, if indeed they exist.

Worse news: there's no practical way to get compensation for injuries. What we British Columbia personal-injury lawyers used to refer to affectionately as "the ICBC pension" whenever we spied that bumper sticker, "Hit me—I need the money," has no Nicaraguan counterpart. Apparently the civil judicial system churns along even more dysfunctionally than the Canadian courts—can you imagine waiting for years for compensation that eventually yields a small pile of *cordobas*? Forget that!

A lawyer and police officer who quickly appeared at the hospital both encouraged me to make an accident report so that the driver would be charged under criminal law. Was there compensation for victims of crime? I asked. No, the only result of such action would be the loss of the driver's job. Or jail. *And another impoverished family*, I thought. So what would be the point? Just more work for lawyers. Judging by the glimpse I had of the driver's stony face as he sat in his truck while the taxi scooped me up, I figured he probably already sported a brown stain on his pants from having hit a tourist. That can't be good for one's driving career.

I would just have to deal with the persistent dizziness myself. Apparently I have a whiplash type of injury to the vertebrae in my neck. It could be worse. Three treatments with a natural medicine practitioner in Leon, at twelve dollars each, helped a lot.

So, here are some tips on crossing the unregulated streets. Crosswalks are seldom if ever indicated and I didn't see a walk light the entire month. The one-ways are not so bad; there are plenty of breaks in traffic. The two-ways can keep you standing on the corner up to five minutes before there's a trustworthy break in traffic. I noticed that some Nicas create their own imaginary crossing several meters or more from the corner, a trick I quickly adopted in deference to the next truck driver wanting to make a sudden turn.

Repeat this mantra as you step onto the streets each day: *I will cross all streets the Nica way. I will wait for big breaks in traffic, for time does not matter. For wherever you go, there you are.*

Wherever you go, life is just better outside the hospital. Take awareness with you into the streets.

Thieves

Unlike some areas in North America, Leon does not present as a drug-soaked city where lurking drug lords and desperate addicts will rob you to fund their next fix or wipe you out if you get in the way of a drug deal. In my recent month there, there was only one news story of a gang-related murder, which seems like an improvement on Vancouver's record. In a way, Leon takes you back in time to a safer, saner, more personal community.

On the other hand, while Nicaragua is said to be the safest country in Central America, is it also said to be the poorest. Poverty breeds pilfering and thefts whose defense is often duress. Nor is the social safety net strong enough to keep old women from needing to beg on the street when they are too old to fetch, haul, carry and cook—I saved all my change for them, thinking, *There, but for the dumb luck of being Canadian, go I.*

An American friend who lives near Leon kept her kitchen locked at night to prevent staff pilfering. I stayed there for a while. One night I goofed and the kitchen was left open for a time. Sure enough, in the morning one of five expensive chocolate bars from home was missing. It had cost me about four dollars in Canada and I reflected that my friend's staff earned perhaps three of those a week. No wonder they supplemented their income!

My friend would generously buy baby clothes for the family's latest newcomer but I would bet the family would rather have the money—or food. That's the level of need at which temptation knocks on people's doors.

Theft happens, apparently a lot. Everyone will caution you about Managua. My ex-pat friend suggested I take a taxi from the airport to my Managua hotel, just across the street, to prevent being mugged while trundling my big fat suitcase over there. Everyone warned us ladies of a certain age about walking around after dark in Granada. (When I saw how many casinos there are in Granada, I could guess that there might be quite a few financially desperate people on the city's streets.) Even in Leon, Dr. Baldizon warned me not to walk after dark near the Riocito, the little river near his office. If we finished treatment after darkness fell, he would call me a taxi whose driver he scrutinized and more or less growled at before letting me step into the vehicle.

So the rumors of rampant theft must be true, eh? In two months in Nicaragua, however, meeting lots of travelers, I did not hear a single authentic tale of robbery or theft, although everyone repeated the cautions.

Of course it makes sense to observe the basic safety rules: don't carry all your valuables with you; have a list of credit-card numbers and telephone numbers in case you lose your cards or documents; stash your valuables in various places so that you don't lose it all at once; stay in reputable hostelries. Certainly, after dark or while ferrying cash to the dentist, I waved down one of those wonderful twenty-cord taxis. I'd sure feel dumb if I was robbed of twelve hundred dollars while trying to save eighty cents!

I did hear one tale of being robbed by an ATM and its bank from a person who then promptly demonstrated how not to follow the instructions on the ATM screen. I wouldn't give that story credence without seeing the evidence. However, ATMs do rob you, indirectly. The limits of daily withdrawal, or per withdrawal, can be ridiculously small, as little as thirty dollars. The biggest daily withdrawal I could find was six hundred dollars, in two transactions, the first for four hundred and the second for two hundred, at the BAC bank. Yet for every foreign withdrawal, your bank at home will probably charge you about five dollars.

My first trip, I reasoned that, in the interests of curbing my spending, I would take out only what I needed for the day, in cords since that's what is used most—until I realized I was paying a five-dollar charge on top of the piddly thirty dollars I took out! My second trip, knowing I'd need cash for the dentist, I withdrew the maximum from a US-airport ATM en route and vowed to find a liberal ATM in Leon. Yet even that six hundred, in two withdrawals, cost me an extra ten dollars—that's 1.7% my bank doesn't deserve!—until I smartened up and took only four hundred each day, cutting the bank's extra fee to 1.25%. The robbers!

I'm still working on this problem. Meanwhile, hang onto any US cash that comes your way, to spend in Nicaragua when the time comes. You can carry up to ten thousand in cash or monetary instruments before the US protests; so carry as much cash as you feel is safe for you.

Sidewalks

Things you need to know about Nica sidewalks:
- They were put there to keep the houses straight, not to facilitate pedestrians.
- Their height above the street may vary from two centimeters to ninety (an inch to a yard, roughly).
- They may round a corner and abruptly stop, with an interesting drop-off or change of scenery.
- They allow houses to bulge out over them at any height.
- Houses may impose impediments onto sidewalks and may install signs, awnings, beams or other outgrowths apparently designed to bonk North Americans of average height on the bean.
- Sidewalk topography displays unrivaled variance in color, texture, level, materials, design, and type of shoe-catcher and toe-stubber.
- They are generally too narrow to walk two abreast, but this consideration will not stop local entrepreneurs from installing an entire underwear shop or toy store on the said sidewalk.
- Squeezing by the shoppers and the clerks is to be viewed as just another interesting travel experience in which you make real contact—inevitably—with the people and you get a change to practise the phrases *Con permiso, me permites,* or *disculpeme, por favor. Excuse me, please,* these phrases mean. Choose one as your mantra of the sidewalks.

Every one of those stalls will be cleared off the sidewalks by nightfall, to reappear magically the next day.

"Come on in! The underwear's fine!" Prepare for a hot time in the old town of Leon tonight with these goodies and those alluring high heels edging the yard-wide sidewalk.

Misdirections

The friendly Nicas would, I think, prefer to die rather than fail to answer your request for directions, even if they haven't the faintest idea where your destination is. They will do their best to help you—except for telling you they don't know what you're talking about.

In Leon this helpfulness is further confounded by the lack of street addresses as those are understood in North America. Houses and businesses do not sport numbers. Streets shyly show their names in tiles mortared into the corner walls—here and there. Most of the time you have no idea what street you are on, which doesn't matter much, since street names are not usually included in directions. The one street in Leon everyone knows is Ruben Diario—it has the bus stops for Poneloya on it, right at the Mercadito (*little market*).

Other than that, get a map and familiarize yourself with all the big churches. The language of churches is big when it comes to giving directions in Leon. A few other landmarks come into play, too, like the hospital, the main square (once it is again habitable), and even the gas station which forms part of my dentist's address on his letterhead! With the churches firmly tacked down in your personal global positioning device and your memory, it's easier to understand directions invariably couched in language like "Three *cuadras* (blocks) south of El Calvario and then right for a block or so until you come to that tree on the left. Yes, the one where the house used to be that horrible bright yellow."

No worries. Any minute now, a taxi driver will come barrelling along who knows where the bright yellow house with the tree was. Those hints are more likely to be useful than the directions, which you, you clever traveler, have figured out from watching the sun on your very first day in Leon, but which seem to make little sense to some drivers.

When Dr. Baldizon gave me the address for the panoramic x-ray, I decided to walk the ten blocks or so. I didn't know where I was going, exactly, but I could always ask for directions, couldn't I?

My first request was a mistake of the worst kind. My direction-giver, a lady selling food at a stall near the market, looked absolutely bewildered before mustering an expression of confidence and giving me exact instructions—in the wrong direction. Belatedly I realized that she probably could not read the paper from the dentist's office. To honor her efforts, I trotted off in the suggested direction until out of sight.

The second request met with similar results, this time one hundred and eighty degrees wrong—from a police officer! I guess he felt the duty to help the public even more strongly, irrespective of whether he knew where things were.

With relief I spied friendly, English-speaking Quetzal Trekkers, and stepped into the relatively cool air of their offices, with quite a sweat on by then, some fifteen blocks later. They straightened me out and off I went to traverse the remaining three blocks.

But the place didn't show up! Did I have crazy pills for breakfast? Bewildered myself by now, I noticed I was in front of the lone art gallery I had found on my previous trip. *The hell with it*, I thought. *X-rays can wait. I might as well have some fun.* In I went to ogle the paintings and there, at the back of the building was the panoramic x-ray office.

Another day, I thought I'd walk to the dentist's office by a new route. I couldn't seem to get back to his street from the new one, however, and every time I asked for directions—you guessed it, the confidently given directions made no sense. Spying a "bikeshaw", I asked once again, thinking anyone who biked people around town for a living must have a map in his head. This young gentleman convinced me that I was, indeed, at the bus station, nowhere near the dentist's office.

Oh, dear. There was no way I could walk back to the dentist's office in time for my appointment. Could he take me over there in the bikeshaw? Sure—for one dollar. Then he looked my portly form over and winced, while his friends giggled behind him.

No doubt he was measuring the effort it would take to get the equivalent of two Nica ladies there. "Two dollars?" I offered, and off we went.

I thought the bikeshaw great fun, offering an entirely new perspective on Leon's streets, especially when we found ourselves in the midst of a funeral procession. I heard my cyclist huffing and puffing, as he himself was a touch on the portly side; in the end he got my sincerest thanks and a fiver. I was only five minutes late.

Now wasn't that fun? You can't really get lost in Leon. If all else fails, grab a taxi or ask a tour company.

Snakes

In spite of staying with a friend in the country and wandering up the jungle paths, I saw only one of Central America's venomous snakes. It was a coral snake, lying on the side of the highway as my friend and I walked along. "Don't step on that," she advised casually. There was no danger, however, as some human before us had found the poor creature and in true Nica style relieved it of its head.

Remember! Not all coral snakes are venomous. Keep this rhyme in mind: *if red touches black, you're ok, Jack; if red touches yellow, you're a dead fellow.* All the same, best to avoid them if you can.

Fear of snakes was the reason I took along one pair of closed shoes. Out in the country, it's nice to know there's a little rubber, leather or polyester between your feet and whatever nasties might lie in wait on the ground, even though I didn't encounter a single one.

Dysentery

Amoebic dysentery, sometimes known as Montezuma's Revenge in Mexico, is apparently quite common, and no big deal. I had it twice during my first trip to Nicaragua, when I stayed on the beach and ate at beachside cafes. The critters didn't take so much as a day out of my life each time.

The first bout coincided with my energetic climb and descent of El Cerro Negro, which shows you how small the effect was. A headache the night before, a little hurling in the morning, a day's fast, and that was it. I took a sample of you-know-what to the lab, had it analyzed, and took a few pills. Cost? One dollar and sixty-five cents.

On the second trip, when I stayed in Leon proper and traveled to three other places, I took an eye-dropper full of black-walnut tincture each day. Not a hint of Montezuma's Revenge all month. Is it the water or the black walnut? Or was I just lucky?

Chileros

Men don't have to worry about this. Women, however, may find themselves suddenly involved in a flirtatious encounter with a man who suggests various kinds of togetherness, usually involving a drink, food, and perhaps entertainment. Just as the fun is getting going, he will reveal that he is, alas, temporarily impecunious. But of course he will make it up to you.

Congratulations. You just hooked yourself a *chilero*.

This happened to me my second or third night out. My own private *chilero* was a handsome guy in his forties who claimed to hold a degree in English and spoke the language well enough for that to be true. He was funny and had a great voice and I did not mind at all buying him beer and munchies. Given the high quality of the entertainment and the low restaurant prices, each of us was getting great value out of this exchange. When he did a spontaneous skit imitating the Spanish of every Latin American country I could name, I nearly fell off the chair laughing.

But My Dinner with Miguel had no dessert: he suggested providing "wild, hot sex". Keeping it light, I replied that even "cold, tame sex" was not on my list of desirable delicacies at present. I sneaked a serious look at him and a great sadness came over me. Sure, I know there are plenty of men eager to get it on with anyone who will stand still long enough, but he didn't strike me as that hormonal. He'd evidently mistaken me for a cougar. What must it take for an educated man to proposition a lumpy woman with bad teeth, twenty years his senior? He must have to say to himself, *It's just business*. He has kids to feed, after all.

His life was neither easy nor admirable. Despite the fun we'd had, I didn't think I could take more of his company. I took leave of him several blocks from my hotel and ducked briefly into La Union in case of being followed. At my age, trust doesn't happen in an hour or two. I breathed a sigh of relief, mixed with sadness, on being let into my beautiful hotel.

Enjoy your *chileros*. But be careful. *Cuidate*.

Are There Downsides?

Return trips

Your dental work might require a return trip. My bone graft, for example, was an unexpected complication which entails a waiting period of nine months. If you're looking for implants, this could happen to you, too. Alternatively, you may not have enough time to do all the work you eventually want done, or you may not have the stamina to do it all in one shot. Maybe you want to see how things go with the first lot of work before plunging for the whole thing.

I look upon this as a perk, a windfall vacation my teeth have given me. For the first time in my life I've found a dentist I can believe in, at prices that won't kill me, and I'm prepared to come back as often as I need dental work as long as this crazy financial situation lasts.

You may never leave

My ex-pat Canadian friend keeps starting sentences in our conversations with the words, "When you move down here…." He is fully invested in Nicaragua and, indeed, may never leave.

I'm beginning to see his point. On my first trip I'd found a six-room beach hotel for ninety thousand dollars and thought it would be a great idea to buy it with friends as a private vacation club. Yet I never envisioned staying in Nicaragua for longer than a vacation or enough time to write a book. On this trip, however, I found places in the mountains cool enough to keep my huge dog, and suddenly possibilities seemed to open up. Property and projects looked more appealing. So who knows? You and I would not be the first North Americans to spend all of our scrawny pensions in Nicaragua.

Will You Be My Guide?

Twist my arm

Thank you for buying this book. It's the sales of books that keep me going. I am not in the business of guiding, advertising, recommending or arranging for travel; I'm just a writer, publisher and educator. The recommendations in this book arise from my own experiences and from meeting so many people from the US and Canada in dire need of affordable dentistry. There may be better hotels, trips, guides, restaurants, or products out there in Nicaragua—if so, I hope to find them on a trip in the future or be told about them by you, my readers.

I love to receive feedback from my readers and your own tips for a wildly successful trip to Nicaragua. When there is enough new material, I'll publish a fresh edition of this book.

If, after reading this little book, you would like to try out Nicaragua and its dentistry with a group or guide, I am open to putting together a trip with like-minded folks. Dr. Baldizon has colleagues in Leon who would welcome the chance to work with North American travelers; so it is feasible for a small group of us to have a toothsome holiday at the same time—we simply need to plan it two or three months in advance.

My next trip to Nicaragua will begin in the last weeks of June, 2013 and will last at least a month. I need only a small amount of the doctor's time to complete the implant and replace a couple of aging (and not-very-well-done) Canadian crowns, which means there's plenty of dental time for you! (There's always plenty of time for you.)

If you would like to come along or meet me in Nicaragua, I'll help arrange overnight arrangements and pick-up in Managua, transport to Leon, accommodations in Leon and, most importantly, dental time! You needn't match your dates to mine; stay as short or long a time as suits you. During the times we overlap, we can have a lot of fun on social occasions or on tours. You'll never get any pressure from me but feel free to ask me to introduce you to all sorts of good and useful people.

If there's enough interest, I'll run a Spanish-in-Three-Days course in Leon to kick off your fun with a new language.

Please let's communicate by email for privacy reasons. Mine is thepackpress@gmail.com.

Toothy Vocabulary

Spanish to English

blanqeamento, el	whitening
boca. la	mouth
cabeza, la	head
corona	crown
cuello, el	neck
dental	dental
diente, el; los dientes	tooth; teeth
dolor, el	pain
drogas, las	drugs
endodoncion, la; las endodonciones	root canal; root canals
extraccion, la; las extracciones	extraction; extractions
farmacia, la; las farmacias	pharmacy; pharmacies
garganta, la	throat
implante, el; los implantes	implant, implants
inferior	lower
inflamacion, la	inflammation
inyeccion, la; las inyecciones	injection; injections
Le duele esto?	Does this hurt?
lengua, la; las lenguas	tongue, tongues
lesion, la; las lesiones	lesion, lesions
mandibula, la; las mandibulas	jaw; jaws
mandibular	mandibular
Me duele [algunos]	[something] hurts
medicamentos	medications
orthodontia, la	orthodontics
pieza, la; las piezas	piece, part, tooth

pildoras, las	pills
por unidad	per unit
porcelana	porcelain
profilaxis	cleaning and protecting
prosthodontia	prosthodontics
radiografia, la; las radiografias	x-ray; x-rays
rayos-x, el; los rayos-x [pronounced *ekkees*]	x-ray; x-rays
receta, la; las recetas	prescription; prescriptions
restauracion, la; las restauraciones	filling; restoration work
saldo pendiente	balance (of your invoice)
sed, la	thirst
superior	upper
trabajo, el	work

English to Spanish

balance unpaid	el saldo pendiente
cleaning of teeth	el profilaxis
crown, crowns	la corona; las coronas
denture, dentures	la dentadura
drugs	las drogas
each; per unit	por unidad
extraction; extrctions	la extraccion; las extracciones
filling; fillings	la restauracion; las restauraciones
hand; hands	la mano; las manos
head	la cabeza

implant; implants	el implante; los implantes
inflammation	la inflamacion
injection; injections	la inyeccion; las inyecciones
It hurts	Me duele
jaw; jaws	la mandibular; las mandibulas
lesion	la lesion; las lesiones
lower	inferior
medication	los medicamentos
neck	el cuello
orthodontics	la orthodontia
pain	el dolor
pills	las piladoras
porcelain	porcelano; porcelana
prescription; prescriptions	la receta; las recetas
prosthodontics	la prosthodontia
restoration; restorations	la restauracion; las restauraciones
root canal	la endodoncion, las endodonciones
thirst	la sed
throat	la garganta
tongue	la lengua
tooth; teeth	el diente, los dientes
upper	upper
whitening	el blanqeamento
work	el trabajo
x-ray; x-rays	la radiografia; las radiografias; el rayo-x; los rayos-x

Resources

Here's my list of twenty-four-carat resources to help you prepare for your adventure in dental tourism in Latin America and to have a wonderful time in Nicaragua.

Managua:

Las Mercedes Best Western Hotel, Managua
book.bestwestern.com

Leon and Las Penitas:

Dr. Juan Carlos Baldizon Chavez
(half-block north and one block east of Texaco Guadalupe)
505-23-11-53-12
drbaldizon@hotmail.com

El Nancite Hotel
(1.5 blocks south of Petronic San Juan)
www.guesthouseelnancite.com
505-88-32-82-40, 505-89-83-00-34,
505-23-15-43-23

Jack the Pirate's Cafetin
(across from Pan Y Paz, one block east)
505-23-11-10-76

Pan y Paz Panaderia Francesa
(One block down—east—from La Union)
505-23-11-10-76

Bigfoot Hostel
www.bigfootnicaragua.com

Green Pathways Tours
www.greenpathways.com

Juan Carlos Fonseca, guide and *taxista*
Transporte Sanchez
505-86-49-24-26
505-23-11-57-46

Tsunami Taco Bar
Across from Hotel Playa Roca on main street of Las Penitas
Google for reviews

Barco de Oro
www.barcodeoro.com

Granada:

Hotel Spa Granada
www.hotelspagranada.com

Hostal Oasis Granada
www.nicaraguahostel.com
oasisgranada@hotmail.com

Choco Museo
www.ChocoMuseo.com

Ometepe:

El Encanto
Carlos Espino
carloselencanto@gmail.com
www.goelencanto.com

Bolivar Espinoza, Guide and *taxista*
Moyogalpa, Ometepe
505-84-30-58-02

Upcountry:

Selva Negra
www.selvanegra.com

See You in Sunny Nicaragua!

Send your queries to the author at thepackpress@gmail.com. I'm happy to answer your letters personally by email.

For more—much more—information on Latin America, Spanish in Three Days, ex-pat living, and just plain good living, you can sign up for Gary and Merri Scott's free newsletter at www.garyascott.com.

If your teeth are bothering you while you're researching your trip, try an extended wash of baking soda to kill the inflammation or use your brush tenderly to apply oil of oregano—or take a painkiller and set a date for getting a new mouth in sunny, friendly Nicaragua!

I feel so much younger and stronger with a fresh, clean, white, *functional* set of teeth that I couldn't wait to pass this miracle on to you by writing this book. Thank you, thank you, wonderful, warm, caring people of Nicaragua for making this possible! Let's keep up the international exchange of goods, skill, and goodwill while helping one another and living the good life meanwhile.

Remember, if a tubby, broke, little old Lady Snaggletooth on her lonesome ownsome can flash a million-dollar smile from Nicaragua for a fistful of dollars, so can you!

Hasta Pronto!

About the Author

Eva van Loon serves as leader of The Pack Press, an independent publisher and publishing-services house in Powell River, BC, Canada. In addition to publishing anthologies, collections, and select non-fiction, The Pack Press offers coaching, high-quality editing, and book production to independent authors and their publishers. The pack supports community publishing and the potent new paradigms arising from the ruins of traditional publishing–what Eva likes to call guerilla publishing. Power to the writer!

After four degrees and careers in teaching, business and law, Eva returned to the education field as a cognition therapist, a new kind of educator whose specialty is fixing learning deficits by re-training the brain. For this professional work, whether with a school district or in private practice, she uses several programs, chief among them the highly successful PACE (Processing and Cognitive Enhancement) program from LearningRX in Colorado. (See www.educare.processingskills.com.) Her dissertation is planned to be a pair of guidebooks to the new field of cognition therapy.

What's most noticeable about Eva is all the dog hair in her life–wolf fur, actually, as she has lived with wolf hybrids for decades. These magnificent creatures seem to enjoy sharing a den with her, where they often serve as editorial assistants, columnists or writers (Eva has to help with the typing as wolfy paws don't do well on the keyboard). Life may a little hairy, but you know they like it that way when you hear the humans and wolves in the household having an exhilarating howling session in the front yard under a big old moon.

She also writes fiction and poetry under the name Kaimana Wolff. You can read about her travelling exploits (with full-color pictures!) at http://www.kaimanawolff.com/

www.ingramcontent.com/pod-product-compliance
Lightning Source LLC
Chambersburg PA
CBHW032150040426

42449CB00005B/461